The New Psychoanalysis

Legacies of Social Thought
Series Editor: Charles Lemert

The New Psychoanalysis

Phyllis W. Meadow

Foreword by Charles Lemert

ROWMAN & LITTLEFIELD PUBLISHERS, INC.
Lanham • Boulder • New York • Toronto • Oxford

ROWMAN & LITTLEFIELD PUBLISHERS, INC.

Published in the United States of America
by Rowman & Littlefield Publishers, Inc.
A wholly owned subsidiary of The Rowman & Littlefield Publishing Group, Inc.
4501 Forbes Boulevard, Suite 200, Lanham, Maryland 20706
www.rowmanlittlefield.com

PO Box 317 Oxford OX2 9RU, UK

British Library Cataloguing in Publication Information Available

Library of Congress Cataloging-in-Publication Data

Meadow, Phyllis W., 1924–
   The new psychoanalysis / Phyllis W. Meadow.
      p. cm. — (Legacies of social thought)
   Includes bibliographical references and index.
   ISBN 0-7425-2824-3 (cloth : alk. paper) — ISBN 0-7425-2825-1 (pbk. :
alk. paper)
   1. Psychoanalysis. I. Title. II. Series.
   BF173 .M3585 2003
   150.19'5—dc21

                                                        2003008297

Printed in the United States of America

⊗™ The paper used in this publication meets the minimum requirements of
American National Standard for Information Sciences—Permanence of Paper for
Printed Library Materials, ANSI/NISO Z39.48-1992.

~

Contents

~

Acknowledgments

To patients, who through their willingness to reveal their true nature led me to the well where I could look in and see myself. They made it possible for me to believe that I could teach the concepts basic to an understanding of the human experience as they are revealed in the psychoanalytic process.

To my students, who gave me the courage to examine the many interpretations of that experience and to search deeper.

To those psychoanalytic training centers—the Center for Modern Psychoanalytic Studies, the Boston Graduate School of Psychoanalysis, and Cyril Z. Meadow Institute—that made it possible to share with analysts-in-training the deeply personal emotional experience provided through the analysis of others.

To Joyce McDougall, the inspiration for this project.

To Charles Lemert, who insisted I go ahead with this project.

To June Bernstein, a remarkable editor, for her many reads and suggestions.

To Ron Lieber, without whose efforts I would never have completed this book.

Finally, to Cy and Dena Meadow for being there.

~

Say Everything!
The Social Imperative?
Charles Lemert

"Say everything!" is the gentle advice a well-trained psychoanalyst gives her patient. The words may differ and are usually not in the imperative, but the instruction remains the same. Without encouragement, the patient who pursues psychoanalytic treatment will never enjoy the benefits of Freud's famous talking cure. Yet, those (myself included) who have spent many years on the couch side of the analytic treatment room realize all too well that the simple encouragement to say whatever comes to mind seldom has the desired effect—at least, not immediately. Entire sessions may pass when what comes to mind is quite beside the point. Truth be told, much of the time one hardly knows what the point is. At times the only thing we know is that we come to the sessions prepared to talk, which often makes it hard to come to the session. Still, we do it as best we can because it was our decision in the first place. At the beginning of an analysis, one agrees to the bare bones contract—the time, the fee, and the principle of saying everything. Appointments are met, mostly; fees are paid, mostly; but, more often than not, the talk is awkward and intermittent.

One can go on like this for years. Then one day (one hardly knows when or why) you realize that you have been talking in these meetings. But to whom? By the time one begins to say everything, you suppose you know your analyst. But what you know are bits and pieces gathered over the years spent staring blankly at the books or art or whatever may be decorating the treatment room. By accident or conniving, you may learn certain facts about her. She may, as mine did years ago, have a baby—a double score. I learned a fact of her life and got to talk to her husband who called the patient list the morning of the delivery. Other details may filter into awareness. Yet, in truth, one hardly knows the person herself at all. For one thing, you never see the analyst except in passing at the appointed hour from door to couch, then fifty minutes later, when you retrace this short but stimulating path.

The benefit of this little game of peek-a-boo is that it allows the patient to develop the all-purpose transference. The analyst may thus become not whoever she is in fact but whomever you need her to be. It is not that she disappears. Quite the contrary, her work is to be there in the most available way possible. She makes herself *emotionally* available even when she keeps quiet. This, it happens, is an act of grace and generosity. To make oneself emotionally available to some other one, whether as an analyst or anyone else, is to take in what he feels. What he feels can in fact be dangerously toxic. It can draw the analyst into disease. I am told that some analysts will not treat depressions because they do not want to get the depressed feeling, which can lead to serious, even morbid, consequences. But the more common, and thus greater, risk to the analyst is the risk everyone takes upon entering a human relationship with the heart wide-open. You get caught in the feelings.

So, think again on the seemingly simple act of encouraging another who has come to you for help. *Say everything!* What appears, at the first, to be laughably innocent turns out to be not only painfully slow to come about but fraught with danger. The analyst, if well trained, deals with the risk recognizing the counter transference—the ways her openness to the patient may stimulate her own unconscious feelings, which can distract from and otherwise trouble the therapy. The patient, by contrast, is relatively defenseless before the risks of the transference. His cure depends on a willingness to take the risk. He knows (even when he does not know why or how) that the whole inconvenient and costly enterprise puts him in danger of having to give up actions, even thoughts, the repetition of which brought him for treatment in the first place.

Hence, the doubled over paradox of the analytic miniworld: A room with only two embodied persons, one seated and one reclined, is soon filled to legal limit with the ghosts of all the others, known and unknown, who have come down into the experience, direct and remote, of the crucial two—the analyst and the analysand. It sometimes gets very crowded. It can be no other way. But that is just the circumstantial paradox. The other ever more practical paradox is that, amid all those ghosts, the two principals must establish and respect a relationship in the face of its impossible conditions. In that the one who comes for help comes because he has had enough of the feelings, thoughts, and behaviors that have made life unbearable, he comes fully armored. The very symptoms that brought him to treatment are the elements of his character he has come to play out to mixed reviews in the worlds of his living. Symptoms stand for (indeed, they *are* in a sense) *both* the cause of suffering *and* the life line to which he clings for survival. Not only does he not know what the symptoms stand for; he may not even know what they are. He just knows that something is terribly wrong.

Hence, the circumstantial and practical paradox turns again, into irony: The simple goal of psychoanalysis is to resolve resistance, beginning with the resistance to the very treatment one seeks in the first place. What is "analyzed," if anything, is first and foremost the resistances—beginning with, remarkably, the resistance to the analysis itself. As Phyllis W. Meadow explains so beautifully in the book you have in hand, the analyst must take care *not* to threaten the patient's defensive attitudes toward *what* (if not quite *who*) he is. And, finally, the irony turns upon itself. One is encouraged to say everything, which is precisely what one cannot do for, were he able, he would not suffer so and thus need to come to a kind person who says, "Say everything!"

As for me, I came to treatment many years ago because, though I did not realize it at the time, I had spent my adult life chasing or otherwise falling for women who, far from merely "not being there," as the saying goes, were actively hostile to me. Some of them I engaged for years on end; others I barely knew. Some I did not know at all—and chief among those I did not know was the lover I had been with (if that is the word) for a number of years. We professed love of the other. Yet, quite apart from refusing ever to make a commitment in the other's direction, we could drive each other crazier than we already were. She once drove away from me, leaving me by the side of a country road. I then ran several miles to my home, got in my car, and chased after her, some hundred miles or so, in order to say whatever I wanted to say, but without the least idea of what she had been feeling so strongly that would cause her to abandon one she believed she loved but did not. We played out dramas of this kind again and again, through many break-ups, and to the astonishment of those few friends we had in common. When it was all over and the tears were shed, I eventually came to realize that the whole thing was two ships passing in the night. She never knew me. I never knew her. Still we wasted some good years of our fading middle lives in some kind of love.

I started the analysis while still in the pain of this relationship, but without understanding why I was in it. I sought a relationship that would go somewhere toward helping with the one that was going so excruciatingly nowhere. I wanted not to feel the pain I had unwittingly made for myself. My analyst was one huge disappointment. She did not look, from what I could tell in the passings, like the girl of my dreams. Not only that but she would not cooperate. She was kind, sympathetic, encouraging, but not in the least seductive. Worse yet, given my *modus operandi*, she was not seducible. Yet, she was to be the one who had to take the place of the girls of my dreams without, of course, ever being a girl in anything more than the dream state of the analytic relationship. For years, I drove more miles to see the analyst than I had to see the girlfriend. At the first, I spent most of my sessions crying when I was not saying stuff that came to mind, much of it persistently beside whatever the point of it all was. It was like living in a world I had helped to create but a world in which the rules made only modest sense, and the activity itself even less. Yet, I kept at it. So did my analyst. We continue even now. Her baby is growing up now. I have married a girl who was never in those dreams and, thus, one who knows and loves me. My wife is not perfect. Nor am I. We have a baby of our own. We have fun. We are often tired. We make love. We have sex. We eat. We cry. Our world is not perfect. I am not cured. But I have a life where none existed before. And on it goes.

What I experience, and now describe, is very much like the good-enough life in society at large. Some live lives ever more tragic than mine. My oldest son, for example, killed himself because his life was filled with miseries he could not comprehend. And others still are so pressed down by the deprivations and assaults of their lives that they don't even rise to the point of despair. Still others, of course, get along just fine without the benefit of treatment. The range of experiences in social worlds can be bewildering. But all lives do have some things in common and these are, curiously, very much like the life lived in the psychoanalytic relationship. Not the same, mind you— *like* it, if not exactly like it. People feel. People don't always know what they feel. People try to say everything. They don't know how. The rules don't make sense. Just the same, we obey them, most of the time, more or less. We want the others in our worlds to be or do everything to and for us. They don't, or they won't. When they try, they fail. Babies come; babies go. You get older. You still live. You keep saying everything. But, then again, you don't.

There is, however, one big difference between life in the psychoanalytic relationship and life outside. And that difference may be all the difference in the world.

Life and work in the psychoanalytic relationship is meant to bring in all of the external and internal realities, such as they may remain. One aims not so much to reconstruct the truth of these realities as to create a little world in which they can be felt and experienced—ultimately, in another of Freud's famous locutions, to work them through. One is encouraged to say everything because the saying-work is a kind of practice, one not entirely different from the Buddhist practice of sitting meditatively in order to practice the experience of the impermanence of life and death. The saying-work, hence the living in the psychoanalytic relation, is thus a kind of practice at saying what comes to mind, which in turn is the work of slowly getting around the resistances to the Say-everything. It is not that the cure produces a character that goes around telling all his secrets, but that in being able to say everything that comes up from the below of the unconscious life one has the option of saying everything because, ultimately, one is willing and able to feel everything. Hardly anyone is ever cured in this absolute sense, and even those who are relapse. I once asked a Buddhist monk who was meditating in a temple why he had a clock in front of him. His reply: So I can know what time it is! However perfectly he meditates, the monk still wants to come back to the present time and to hold it. Likewise, the cured patient is drawn back to the normal human state of not saying everything because some things, if said, are frightening—and not necessarily to those who hear them, but to the one who might say them. And there, precisely, is the difference between the miniworld of the analytic relationship and the so-called real world of life in society. Life with others—with, that is, the many and entire worlds of others, too numerous to know or even to count—is a world in which one *must* not say everything. Such a statement seemingly betrays a profound lack of respect for the very democratic values professed by most, if not all, so-called modern societies.

The democratic ideal is that *everyone* has a voice. Leave aside, for the time being, the sad but true reality that in most parts of the globe colonized by alleged democracies the aspiration to this ideal is weak (at best) and in some cases nonexistent (save when applying for World Bank funds). What counts is that in modern or postmodern societies, some or another version of the democratic ideal is held up as a standard for civil participation. In practical terms, even those societies, like the American one, that approximate the ideal in their institutional arrangements, do not achieve it so much as give it lip service. Rights to due process, *habeas corpus*, competent legal representation, among others, are suspended, legally or not, on a regular basis. The technical right to free speech, while protected in principle, is withdrawn at the crucial moment of personal jeopardy. Even when those rights are untouched by those in formal authority, it can hardly be said that the fabled modern state has been a social environment in which the voice of the people regularly governs. Not even the more optimistic of liberal theorists of modern politics will grant that the people have voice, at most, by the trust they invest in their elected representatives. It hardly need be said that, apart from the failure of the electoral process in most modern nation-states, those elected to represent a constituency do so at best through the oblique means of direct lobbying and indirect polling results. At worst, the representatives represent no more than a thin layer of the most neighborly members of their own social strata—those, that is, with whom they talk and listen most comfortably.

Still the democratic ideal is interesting when set against the psychoanalytic ideal of saying everything. In principle, a social and political democracy is a complex, but concrete, social arrangement in which the people (the *demos*) are meant to rule by virtue of their freedom to say everything. This, of course, is (even at its best) a kind of ruse. Not even in the pure and original Greek polis did all the elders of the forum say everything. Nor, today, do members of the British Parliament (literally, the British speaking body), perhaps the most intimate and intense speaking institution there is, though it would seem that nothing constrains members from shouting or hissing at what is being said by those who do speak. Yet, even in the House of Commons, a relatively small room, the back-benchers are seldom called on. In the exterior world of actual and complicated social institutions saying everything is, one can safely say, *never* achieved, even when the ideals of those institutions teach members to *believe* that it can be.

Nor do other institutions committed to the unrestrained voice. The modern university is founded on the right of free inquiry—hence, the right of free speech. Yet, anyone who has recently been a student or teacher in one of them realizes that one cannot say everything—neither as a teacher, nor as a student, nor as a participant in the nether regions of college social life. You can get called up on all sorts of charges that make no sense at all. In fact, in the academy the freedom to speak and write is always a *disciplined* freedom—hence, the practical (if not first) meaning of the ideal of the academic disciplines. Teachers train students as they were trained—*not* to say everything but to say (and to write) according to the literatures and other discursive traditions of the discipline in which they are, or they seek to be, certified. Likewise, in addition to the democratic parliament and the free university, the Protestant sects were established precisely in order to assure religious freedom to pursue the word of God for themselves. Yet, it hardly need be said that your local Protestant church is anything but a place in which one might speak freely. Whether the local sect is a liberal one, like the Quakers or Unitarians, where the Word is meant to steal silently into the heart of the congregants or a more evangelical one where the norm is to roll and shout according to the promptings of a holy ghost, what one says or shouts is still strictly reined in by the social norms that have little in common with the freedom to say or shout just anything.

One might, in the search for a public institution where saying everything has a place, come to the family. But here, quite apart from the reality that most families are broken and frequently tyrannical, the ideal of the family haven has never taken hold, even (and especially) in its hey-day of the post-war 1950s in America. Phyllis Meadow, in her discussion of violence, recalls the postwar show tune from *South Pacific* and its words: "You got to be carefully taught to hate." Her reference is striking because the song was a hit at precisely that moment when the idyllic family was thought to have been, at least among affluent whites, the evident norm. Yet, even then, hatred was carefully taught, not so much in the schools, as in the families, as fathers brought home stories of the "Japs" in the South Pacific to complement the local folklore on "Niggers." One hardly need mention the terrifying statistical accounts of the cases of family violence, many of them unreported. In the reality of real social worlds, there are at best only occasional and short-lived havens where individuals can say everything. Hence, the significant difference between life in the social out-of-doors and life in the privileged sanctuary of the treatment room. Life outside the miniworld of psychoanalysis is more treacherous still. Violence is the unspoken norm that thrives under the cover of the empty *everythings* said by politicians, preachers, professors, and parents who profess the unattainable ideals. Inside the analyst's office, there are risks in saying what comes to mind, but here the analyst and the patient enter into their awkward accord that requires the one to protect the other so what comes to mind *might* be said, even when it mostly is not. The psychoanalytic miniworld is not a democracy, thank God! You get one vote—to enter according to the rules or not. You may break the rules, of course, but the violations are subject to talk and, if habitual, may lead to the suspension of civil rights. Nor is it, of course, a dictatorship (though I am told that some analysts run their practices according to a presumption of their absolute authority to interpret the words).

Still, of all the theoretically free social institutions in modern society—civil society, the religious institutions, the family, the press and media, the universities—none is so thoroughly free, in the sense of being protected in fact and in principle from the intrusions of the wider world as the psychoanalytic room. Not even, one is reminded, the physician's and the lawyer's communications are as privileged (if only because the psychoanalytic relation is so long-enduring that it would be perilously difficult for a snoop to figure out when and where some incriminating word was said, and what it meant). This is a little surprising, in one sense, because a good many analysts do their work in and around psychoanalytic institutes where, in effect, many of the patients, and their analysts, are also in training analysis or supervision (and sometimes group analysis) with other members of the institute community. They talk about each other and each other's "material" in *their* analytic or supervisory sessions. In effect, the unique feature of the psychoanalytic institute, sociologically speaking, is that it is the one institution in modern societies where the rule of confidentiality is so strictly regarded and, yet, in spite of this, so vulnerable to inspection. In effect, patients treated in these places come to trust their analysts to keep the confidence, which they do. Names are never revealed. Ethical analysts never even confirm that so-and-so is a patient. Yet, in institutions and treatment centers where everyone can see who enters or leaves this or that office, people guess and decide. It is in the nature of the analytic relationship that one feels labile and thus open to inspection even by outsiders. Though identities and details are protected, the analytic talk does end up, however disembodied, in the analytic narratives of others—if only in the supervisory sessions the analyst may have or the case presentations she makes in order to improve her skills. Then there is the inevitable force of human curiosity. We who have had sessions in institutes just assume we know who the cases presented might be. Most of the time, we are dead wrong. Sometimes we guess correctly, but these guesses are themselves taken for what they are—as symptoms of our feelings, not facts of some other patient's.

I have my own guesses about several of the cases Phyllis Meadow describes in *The New Psychoanalysis*. I am a gossip and a snoop like everyone else. But, when I am practicing the gains of my own analysis, I ask myself, "Now why do I think that case applies to X? [where X, far from being the person I guess at, may actually be myself]." Still, it remains that the work of saying everything in session may include the pleasures and pains of speculating about all the others one supposes to be in like situation. Strange as it may seem, the stories of our inner lives are different only in nuance and detail. The stories themselves are disconcertingly similar, which is why we try so to link ourselves to others, if only to prove to ourselves that we are not *that* bad.

Psychoanalytic relationships are not just crowded with the fantastic others brought into the analytic talk in treatment. They also are, in effect, part of an imaginary community of shared dreams and other reported materials that filter through the confidences into the clinical papers, supervisory sessions, and all the other things said in such a place—not to exclude the normal run of gossip. Analysts and analysands are talkers. Accordingly, the psychoanalytic world is a world of talk. This is the one point everyone gets. This, in turn, may be what makes the psychoanalyst a subject of intrigue among writers, filmmakers, and the general public. One supposes there is something unusual going on in there, and they are right. What is going on is that, in a peculiar way, though the miniworld of the treatment is very, very tiny, it is a setting into which the whole wide world is peering. It is in effect the one place where the realities of worldly experience enter normally without actual consequence. That, precisely, is the social value of the ideal of a world in which everything takes place in talk. The *saying-everything* is the way of living in these worlds. Though there are phonies and bastards everywhere, including here, in the long run no one pretends this world is anything more than this.

To some, including those already familiar with the experience, this may seem an oddball tangent. But, I think, it is far more than a clever observation. The reality of analytic worlds is that they are places where the contradictions of the allegedly real world present themselves in all their force, if (generally) without violent consequence. Violence happens of course. I know of fist fights, suicides, sexual transgressions, and clinical deaths occurring in institutes between analysts and their patients. Still, and in spite of these deviations, the analytic world is the one place where the rules are few but strictly to be obeyed, and obeyed ultimately not because of the threats of the rule keeper but by the will of the patient who seeks the treatment. In many short runs, even these little worlds do not work according to their own principles, but in the long runs they do; thus, they are the one and perhaps only continuing social relationship in which there is a chance that everything that needs to be said *might* be said—in which there is an unfettered, equalitarian access to the truth of human experience. This exceptional fact of the psychoanalytic relationship is why, no doubt, it has, from time to time, served as a model for the critique and social reform of real, external social republics.

It is not surprising that the tradition of social theory that most frequently resorts to Freud is one whose members suffered, as did Freud himself, as subject to the rise of Hitler and the regime of National Socialism in Germany and eventually Europe generally. The German school of critical theory—from Eric Fromm to Herbert Marcus to Jürgen Habermas—has done more to bring psychoanalytic principles into social theory than any other single tradition with the possible exception of the French poststructuralists, including Jacques Lacan as well as Michel Foucault and Jacques Derrida. Either way, it had to have been Europeans who lived through the ravages of Hitler and World War II who would have thought to have turned the theory of social realities inside out in order to investigate the dark inscrutabilities of the unconscious. Whatever else the Nazi terror was, it was, in actual social history, the principal and most devastating assault on the democratic ideal. That ideal is, we seldom admit, fragile at best, for it relies on the unreliable belief that the people who rule can and will say everything, and that what they say counts, even when what they say, when they say something at all, is said by feeble acquiescence to the rules. We get the rulers we deserve. Hitler's rise to national power in 1933 was by legal means. His terror was joined by the German people—not because they were terrorists but because, among other reasons, everything he said was said so very well that, at first hearing, one could hardly resist the thrill of it all. Then too, Hitler's genius was that he said things about Jewish and other non-Aryan people that many in Germany and throughout the West felt but would never say in public. The violence the Nazis made into an organizing principle of the Third Reich corresponded to the violence within—not just among Germans but all moderns.

Outside the psychoanalytic world, saying everything is a different kind of risky business. Inside, you have only your resistances to lose. Outside, you can lose your life, or your livelihood, or your friends and families. This difference, among the others, may be why, in spite of the Freud bashing and ill-informed (or, one might say, HMO-informed) attacks on psychoanalytic treatment, there remains a rather robust romanticism of the psychoanalytic relationship on the part of those, especially the German theorists, who think deeply and critically about what is needed in the world at large.

You cannot do psychoanalysis as a romantic, at least not in the long run. But this does not prevent anyone who stands outside the relationship from seeing in it the principles that might well serve the dirty worlds in which they live, if only . . . The "if only" here is the conditional disenchantment of the dream of the pure, free world of human relations. To say "if only" is to hold out for the possibility that, though the odds are slim, one might find a way—in this case, a way to instill in the larger world the conditions and possibilities that pertain in the psychoanalytic world. Who would not want to cure the social world, if a cure could be had?

There, precisely, is the rub. It may well be that the necessary social imperative is respect for the healing effects of saying everything. From time to time, there are political leaders with the courage and wisdom to do just this. In our time, Vaclav Havel, the leader of the Czech revolution against communist rule and for years the president of the Czech Republic, shocked the world by his unorthodox manner as well as his brute honesty. The key to Havel's success as a political leader was not, however, his literary brilliance or even his humble manner—both of which were occasionally lost on his followers and opponents. The key to his moral leadership may have been his words upon leaving office early in 2003, when, among other things, he apologized to those who hated him for having let them down. He asked their forgiveness! The words were neither obsequious apologies nor contrived honesties. They simply addressed the underlying reality of politics. Some people love their leaders; others hate them. The body politic has both feelings, neither of which is alien to the other. Havel was saying for everyone the Everything of political reality. He said what anyone with her wits about her knows to be true of real social worlds: *that we fail, as we succeed; that we injure, as we heal; that we lie, as we seek the truth; that we destroy, as we try to build up.*

This is the discovery that Freud announced in 1920 when he settled into the dual drive theory that governed his thinking for the remainder of his days. It is no accident, one supposes, that he came to the idea when he did. The reason Europeans refer insistently to World War I as the "Great War" is that it was *the* war in which the naïve faith of modernity definitively collapsed. The Nazi reign of terror was still in the offing. But the failure of democratic will that led to the Great War was a nightmare to those who had hoped, along the troubled nineteenth century, that modern democratic principles in concert with modern industrial capitalism would at long last lead to genuine human progress and, eventually, to the Good Society, modernity's dream of an earthly paradise. Immanuel Wallerstein describes the two world wars of the twentieth century as one continuous war between Germany and the British, French, and reluctant American allies. The Peace of Versailles, settled in 1919, the year before Freud's "Beyond the Pleasure Principle," was so grotesquely punitive toward Germany that anyone with eyes to see could see that the peace would not last.

Whether or not Freud studied politics as closely as he did literature is not clear (though Peter Gay, perhaps Freud's most accomplished biographer, suggests that he did). But, this possibility aside, Freud had to have seen the effects of the Great War on his patients and colleagues, not to mention himself. It was, thus, a perfectly evident, if tragic, conclusion for him to have come in such times as those: to believe that human nature is driven by two, equally strong, but tension producing, forces—the one toward life, the other toward death; the one toward constructive work, the other toward destruction. In short, what Freud saw, whether from the clinical or historical records (or both), was that we do not say everything because we are torn between these two opposing forces.

Among psychoanalysts active today, Phyllis Meadow is one of the foremost proponents of dual drive theory. She is also a visionary, as well as a life force herself. Sociologists will be amused, perhaps pleased, to learn that she once was a research assistant to C. Wright Mills. I have never, myself, been able to verify the precise influence Mills or sociology may have had on her thinking.

But I can give witness to sociological wisdom in her actions. Among *clinical* psychoanalysts, few have seen, as Meadow has, the importance of using psychoanalytic insights to attack the foremost symptom of modernity's quite shocking character disorder: social violence. Whether sociologically or not, Meadow has founded (in addition to three analytic institutes in Boston, Vermont, and New York City) the Institute for the Study of Violence at the Boston Graduate School of Psychoanalysis, which offers training in sociology and neurobiology as well as psychoanalysis.

Phyllis Meadow's *The New Psychoanalysis* is, thereby, one of the surest guides one could find to the vast social as well as clinical implications of the dual drive theory of Freud's mature years. She calls her tradition "modern psychoanalysis" so as to distinguish it from traditional, more intellectualizing practices that owe to Freud's early thinking. I have long thought that the tradition should be called "postmodern psychoanalysis" (but it is far too late to change the name). The perspective is, if not *postmodern*, at least outside-the-modern—otherwise it could not have the critical leverage it does toward the modern way of violence.

Anyone thoroughly immersed in the modern world has little perspective from which to judge its most insidious contradiction—that of thinking of itself as the one progressive and humanistic social arrangement in the whole of human history, while being in fact and reality just as violent and destructive as any other. The fabled Greeks who invented the democratic ideal were also warriors. The Americans and the British, among the more high-minded of the modern civilizations, claim the same high standard of respect for human values, when in fact they have been among the most ruthless colonizers ever. That they colonize in superficially civilized ways does not make their colonizing any less ruthless. Just ask the poor in India or Pakistan, not to mention Kashmir, or in the Middle East; or ask the Lakota in South Dakota or the rural peasants in the Philippines. Gandhi's famous quip is to the point: What did he think of British civilization? "It would be a good idea." The same applies to all the modern nation-states. Modern societies think of themselves as better than the rest. In some (mostly material ways) they are. But in the reality of lived experience they are every bit as violent as any other civilizational ideal. It is a well-known fact that the most violent century in human history—as measured by the numbers of persons suffering from war, civil strife, massacres, urban and rural violence, wanton slaughters, and violent crimes—is the twentieth; and the twenty-first is off to a good start at breaking the record.

Late in life, Freud made an attempt to apply his dual drive theory to the social world at large, most famously in "Civilization and Its Discontents" (written in 1930, a decade after the turn to drive theory, but also at the beginning of the nightmare decade for Germany and Europe). That essay, though interesting for what it promises as a sociological extension of his principles, has always struck me as more of a lament than a serious analysis of the problem at the structural foundations of modern societies. In one of the book's more famous passages, Freud extended his dual drive theory to the world writ large:

> The meaning of the evolution of civilization is no longer obscure to us. It must present the struggle between Eros and death, between the instinct of life and the instinct of destruction, as it works itself out in the human species. This struggle is what all life essentially consists of, and the evolution of civilization may therefore be simply described as the struggle for life of the human species. And this is the battle of the giants that our nurse-maids try to appease with the lullaby about Heaven.

On the one hand, especially in the poetic denunciations of the last sentence, it would be difficult to find a more compelling critique, not so much of religion but of the lullaby of modernity itself—the silly dream of the modern world as one of freedom and human fulfillment. On the other, Freud's dual drive scheme is taken, without sufficient revision, from the clinical setting where it appears so clearly (if not manageably) to its application to the decay of modern society as such. The leap is not that easy to make.

Yet, it is the leap that must be taken, again and again, until we get it right. What is so terribly flawed about the allegedly free institutions of modern society, not to mention their vapid principle of democratic rule, is that they serve not to liberate but to enslave. The other great analyst of the hidden contractions of the modern world, Karl Marx, made this point a good half-century before Freud got it right. Yet, Marxisms of all kinds suffered the equivalent and obverse limitations of Freudianisms of most kinds. The former locate the evil of the modern world in the economic exploitation of workers in the name of free labor markets. The latter locate it in the essential instincts of life itself—in, effectively, a kind of metaphoric biology. Both are correct to a good degree. The modern world does enslave by economic exploitation. But, also, the modern world is about the forceful will to life. Both Marx and Freud say that things are not what they present themselves to be. Both allow for the long duration of the human struggle between constructive and destructive forces. But neither gives a satisfactory account of the breach between the large structural forces of society and the local bodies and psyches in which the no less large (if hard-to-stipulate) instincts play xxii ⁓ Series Editor's Foreword

out their tensions, contradictions, and death-dealing violence—all in the name of life.

The striking thing about Marx's solution was that it has been tried and does not seem to work. The socialist revolutions came sporadically. Most were reversed in a short time, as in 1848 and 1871, perhaps also in places in 1968. Where they took hold as in Russia, China, Cuba, Angola, and Ghana, among other places, they soon fell under the spell of the same sort of lullaby Freud calls attention to—the heaven of a pure socialism of freedoms and equalities that never came to pass and, most devastating to the socialist lullaby, never came close to providing for the material needs of the proletariat.

By contrast, the no less striking thing about the psychoanalytic solution is that it has never even been tried. The modern world places such forceful strictures on the right to *say-everything* that the occasions when and where such a radical idea may have had the upper hand—in the wider social world—are few and far between. Many take the revolutions of 1968 as a passing instance thereof. There is something to be said for this. From the free speech movement in Berkeley to the events of *Mai '68* in Paris, there were a few short weeks of public freedom to say the truths that were long oppressed. But these events lasted no longer than the revolutions of 1848 and were soon reversed by repressive forces. But, like the revolutions in Cuba and the Soviet Union, they soon played themselves out of their own accord. Surely the idea of *saying-everything* has to do with more than shouting "Fuck you!" at the Berkeley cops or throwing bricks at the French gendarmes.

Say everything! Could it be the necessary social imperative? Could it be the one social practice that if repeated again and again would allow the social whole to work through its own interior struggle with life and death? Given the record of other experiments in this direction, one could well consider it as possible. Is the talking cure applicable in civil society? All one can say is that this was the original and pure ideal—that the free citizenry, gathered in well-protected public associations, guarded by First Amendment rights to free speech would and could remake the social whole into the good society. Civil society, in its pure form, was meant to be that ideal social space between the state (which will always follow its own narrow and ruthless interests) and the isolated individual (who, in the interest of self preservation, is defenseless before the state powers).

The civil society ideal is not quite the ideal of the psychoanalytic chamber. For one thing, it has proven painfully difficult to hold to the rules—to encourage, that is, the kind of talk that assures sufficient civility so that the participants in the free civil sphere can say, and think, and feel everything. For another, in the Americas especially, the various Christian Puritanisms have made it nearly impossible to speak of human desires in the rich unfettered and *even* (if not simply) sexual sense. This is why, among a long list of moral crimes against human freedom, the one social group in modern societies most commonly subjected to verbal and physical violence are those who dare to violate the heterosexual norms. Not only are the rates of violence against gays and lesbians extraordinarily high, but the long history in America of violence against black men, in particular, is well known to be aggression against their sexual being.

The say-everything imperative deserves a hearing and, on the surface, would likely be worth the practical effort. At the least, we know that the first right to be withdrawn—either formally or furtively—is the right to free speech. In times of war, or approaching war, one simply cannot say everything without a risk. And those who do, those whose names and number we shall never know, are thrown into prisons or pits.

Phyllis Meadow's *The New Psychoanalysis* is, in my view, among the most readable resources there is to the clinical evidence for the psychoanalytic process. Psychoanalysts not of her persuasion will learn from arguing with her, as analysts do. Students, including those in colleges as well as psychoanalytic institutes, and not a few patients, will learn exactly what the modern psychoanalytic method is, and why it is. And social theorists, as well as others not primarily students or practitioners of psychoanalysis, will also benefit from reading a very wise and imaginative clinician's account of the social value of respect for human feelings and emotional communications—those basic methods of the analytic relationship that allow for the saying of everything, which in turn can establish a new social relation, in which real, as opposed to theoretical, human freedom holds the world in its hand.

CHAPTER ONE

~

The New Psychoanalysis

Then and Now

The reader may wonder what could be new about psychoanalysis. When Freud (1893) told patients to say everything that occurred to them, psychoanalysis was born as a separate and distinct profession. It ceased to be a medical treatment and became a verbal one interested in understanding human emotion.

Freud's definition of psychoanalysis has stood the test of time. It is a body of knowledge on mental and emotional functioning, a theory of treatment technique, and an approach to research.

In the first two decades of the last century, Freud experimented with techniques from hypnosis to the laying on of hands. All of the techniques used in early psychoanalytic work were based on the concept of repression, the idea that a person's desires have been exiled from conscious thought. Psychoanalysts were concerned with such questions as what motivates a person to behave in ways that seem irrational or that lead to low self-esteem or failure to achieve conscious goals. A patient may insist that he cannot do what he wants. Matters are out of his control. It seems a schism exists between what a patient says he wants and what his behavior tells us he is seeking.

The analyst takes it as her task to elaborate the mental and emotional causes behind an individual's conscious ways of thinking and perceiving the world. This work involves restoring forgotten desires to consciousness. The theory behind this work is that a motivational force that shapes behavior and influences thought and feelings resides outside a person's awareness. Psycho-analysts were able to build a model for their observations around this moti-vation theory, a model that enabled them to make predictions about the be-havior, thinking, and perceptions that a patient could be expected to display in future sessions.

This kind of treatment is based on a further premise that there is a rela-tionship among the images an individual sees in his mind, forces within his body, somatic pathways that these forces travel, and motor behavior.

In his "A Project for a Scientific Psychology," Freud (1895) insisted that psychoanalysis is a science. Later philosophers of science, such as Grünbaum (1984), were skeptical of a science based on the recovery of repressed psychic material from an unconscious. Academic researchers gave up on tracking the contents of the unconscious in favor of investigations of measurable concepts that could be viewed as "scientific." They left the field of the unconscious to clinical psychoanalysts.

When Freud (1916–1917d) recognized the strength of a counterforce to "knowing" one's own impulses, the emphasis shifted from making the un-conscious conscious to the study of resistances that prevent an individual from knowing his thoughts and feelings. Then resistance analysis took prece-dence over deeper probing of the unconscious.

By 1920, the dual drive theory with its acknowledgment of two separate sets of drives, the erotic and the aggressive, raised many questions about the role of defense, the structure of the mind, and the relation between drives and behavior. After Freud's publication of "The Ego and the Id" and "Beyond the Pleasure Principle," the contents of the unconscious were clarified.

Has anything new happened in psychoanalysis since then?

There were many controversies in the twenties and thirties, particularly around the idea that from birth humans struggle with drives to build and drives to tear down in their attempt to manage stimulation. Consideration of these endogenous forces led to the view that when destructive tendencies were gaining control over life's constructive drives, action was inhibited, and anxiety was aroused. Freud (1920) argued for the existence of opposing life and death drives. Then psychoanalysts debated the validity of a theory that presumed a death instinct innate in all human beings. Despite intense con-flicts between schools of analytic thought, one valuable result arose from these debates. This new concept of dual drives, including an aggressive com-ponent, rendered possible the treatment of emotional conditions previously considered inaccessible to psychoanalysis because of what had been termed "the stone wall of narcissism." Narcissism could be conceptualized in terms of destructive rather than libidinal drives, which led to further work on severe character disturbances, borderline conditions, and, eventually, psychosis and the perversions.

The difficulty inherent to narcissistic individuals in forming personal relationships with those experienced as different from the self led analysts to explore causes of merger, separation, and isolation. Analysts became interested in why it was so difficult for some children to separate from their early caretakers and give up the omnipotence and superiority of this oneness in order to function with others in relationships.

Recognizing the universality and developmental roots of narcissism in our nature, psychoanalysts set as their goal to "breach the wall" in order to make contact with the narcissistically regressed person. The earlier emphasis by psychoanalysts on sexual (erotic) drives delayed the investigation of destructiveness and aggression in the personality and, more specifically, how the two sets of drives interact to create the dramas of our lives.

Case presentations moved in a new direction. In Freud's (1905b) original libido theory, destructiveness and aggression were considered the outcome of thwarted sexuality. After dual drive theory and a search for a cure of narcissism was undertaken, analysts understood that when destructive impulses are denied satisfactory outlets, an individual's potential for creativity is limited. Toward the end of his life, Freud (1937a) pondered why he had for so long overlooked the significance of aggression in character formation.

Anna Freud (1953) suggested that the instincts, including aggression, serve as mind builders. The achievement of love and mature sexual function as humanistic ideals gave way to an appreciation of the role of aggressive urges in the development of mind and in the mature character structure. The fact that a group of aggressive drives presses for discharge was understood as a motivational force in creating awareness of the outside world. The cognitive search to use and store experiences could be seen as one way to achieve satisfaction of aggressive drives.

Nevertheless, many analysts continued to reject the concept of innate destructiveness, insisting that aggression only results from the frustration of libidinal drives. This meant that frustration coming from outside the body could be thought of as the cause of destructiveness. Over time, however, most analysts recognized the work of destructive drives as equal to that of the life (sexual) drives. The impulse to undo and destroy life was seen to be an integral part of the developmental process. Clinical material revealed how persistently patients try to escape internal pressure for the discharge of destructive drives.

Deeper understanding of impulsiveness has led to new approaches to murderous feelings, envy, possessiveness, and pathological competition. Analysts now recognize that in health aggressive impulses may be employed to further goals of the life drives, and analysis can work toward this fusion. Certain pathologies, such as lack of intellectual curiosity, sexual impotence, weak emotional attachments, and warring emotions toward loved objects, could be understood as a failure to achieve drive fusion. Dual drive theory clarified why we of necessity feel love and hate toward the same person. Negative feelings are not just a reaction to frustration of one's wishes by the mother; spontaneous aggression exists from birth toward the very person to whom one turns for satisfaction. Aggression is a spontaneous response to being alive.

Following World War II, the major diagnosis in Veterans Administration hospitals was schizophrenia. Psychotic defenses could be examined over larger populations. Detachment, isolation, and delusional states were more clearly connected to the fear of consequences of acting on one's own aggressive impulses. Answers were sought in genetic, constitutional, and environmental research projects.

In the early 1950s, schizophrenic children and their parents treated in the Bronx office of the Jewish Board of Guardians were studied under a federally funded grant. These studies indicated that when the need is aroused to rely on something or someone, so, too, is the wish to destroy and detach from longings. Some of the children were able to merge with a powerful figure and thus eliminate feelings of emptiness and need. Those children who denied the need for another failed to recognize that they existed separately from the needed caretaker. The wish to take possession of, or demean, a powerful caretaker could generate the individual's detachment from all longings, including the need to be cared for. This detachment, combined with blocked awareness of other persons, could result in the schizophrenic reaction to impulses. In treating narcissism, analysts learned that what the world was calling narcissism was similar to the infant's response to internal disturbances. An overstimulated infant can go to sleep as a way of detaching itself from stimulation. Similarly, a patient frightened by his helplessness blots out the world around him as he enters a detached, self-preoccupied state.

By the mid-1950s, modern analysts were beginning to take cases into treatment that appeared impossible to reach. As part of their psychoanalytic education, students of modern analysis spent time studying patients in mental hospitals. They were asked to consider such questions as "What motivates a person to give up living in the real world?" Many doubts existed about how to help severely disturbed veterans and other mental hospital patients. Even after some success treating psychotic and borderline cases, questions lingered about the legitimacy of long-term treatment of patients who talked word salad and seriously disguised their communications. How could one attempt a "talking cure" with such patients?

In the absence of emotionally significant language, analysts had to develop means of communication that would lead to an emotional understanding of the patient's unique experience. It was particularly necessary to know what was being communicated through body symptoms, irrational behaviors, and delusional states. What was most striking about patients in mental institutions was the level of deprivation and neglect they tolerated. Most hospital personnel could not relate to detached patients who could not carry on meaningful communications. After our students learned to establish a nonintrusive relationship in which the desire for distance was respected, some of the patients reached out to them, asking, "Are you my doctor? Are you here to see me?" Most patients wanted the visitor to give them something. "Do you have any cigarettes?" they would ask. "Give me a dime. Buy me a Coke, a cup of coffee."

I once treated Barry, a severely depressed man, who asked for nothing more than not to be pressured. It was clear that imposing ideas that Barry had not thought was experienced as pressure. After some time with him, I learned that by never asking for anything, he could retire into his depressive position of feeling neglected. In his view, I was the person who had no concern for him, who neglected him, and he felt vindicated by the proof that these feelings about me could be verified.

Similarly, it was found that when a student tried to satisfy a hospitalized patient's requests, the patient lost interest in the therapist and dismissed or ignored him. This led to a recognition of the persistence of the search for a depriving object who bears out the patient's belief that he is neglected, unwanted, and unloved.

Each patient responds somewhat differently. One becomes indifferent while another becomes a bottomless pit demanding ever more. When not given what he demands, the patient may rage, speak in garbled language, or become abusive. Often analysts feel frightened by the behavior of severely disturbed patients. When analysts had the same feelings repetitively with particular patients, they learned to use their feelings to ask questions or make statements that led to the patients feeling understood. Acceptance eases the patient's concerns about his own impulses. An analyst might simply ask the patient, "Should I be afraid?"

When one practices psychoanalysis with the conviction that there is an innate urge to destroy, it allows for an acceptance of patients' destructive impulses that may lead to appropriate discharge in the treatment. This, in turn, permits patients to experience loving feelings. Over time a psychotic patient can learn to tolerate the feelings that are aroused in him. The feelings induced in the analyst by psychosis clue us into what the patient cannot tolerate within himself.

In the 1960s, 1970s, and 1980s, answers were sought in child development studies. In those years enormous progress was made in knowledge of infant development. While these studies did not constitute psychoanalytic research, the results supported many of the clinical findings of psychoanalysis.

Why Is the Patient in My Office?

Even in the analysis of milder cases, to define pathology and to think about cure, analysts have first to consider the data of psychoanalysis—that is, what patients talk about during sessions. When invited to talk, verbal patients present their problems in living. They discuss how they cope with frustrations; they describe their hopes, their fantasies, perhaps, their dreams. They tell the analyst their memories of important people in their lives, and they try to describe how they relate to others and how others relate to them. In other words, they convey to the analyst the known facts of their lives.

How the analyst listens is important. The analyst will get to know a patient by how he himself thinks and, more important, feels about the patient he is with.

For the purposes of conducting psychoanalysis, the content of the patient's life will not tell the analyst as much as will the feelings that the analyst has when with the patient in the sessions. Factual content of an individual's life tends to represent his defensive story line. What is presented is as if I were the person I am describing. That is the big "I" talking, but the patient induces feeling states in the analyst that tell more about his emotional conflicts than do his stated opinions. From the induced states the analyst can generalize about the patient's self-image.

Analysts differ significantly in the model used for listening. In recent years, two major approaches have dominated. One is to attend to the patient's experience as he relives and reenacts it in the here and now—in other words, to study his characterological responses to internal and external stimulation in the presence of an analyst. Many analysts have moved to this "live" model in which the patient's style of being, expressed in the transference relationship, is the primary source of data for understanding the patient. In this model the analyst is interested in what the patient longs for in the treatment situation itself, instead of what he reports about outside relations. What is most significant is how he defends against knowing his longings when they are aroused and what he does when disappointed. As he describes his outside life, he reveals how he colludes with others to defeat himself. These same strategies will arise in the transference both to defeat the analyst and the analysis. The reader may have the impression that this is only true of seriously disturbed patients, but that is not the case. Patients who appear fairly well adjusted but seek help because life is holding back something are equally likely to cling to their self-defeating behaviors.

Not all analysts have adopted this method of understanding the patient. Ego analysts attempt to establish a connection between current emotional problems and childhood experiences, while the hermeneuticists try to work out a story line, together with the patient, that explains behavior and defensive methods employed by their patients.

Schools of Psychoanalysis

With advances in neuroscience in the past twenty years, modern analysts have reemphasized unconscious motivation, again turning their attention to the hidden purposes that exist when the individual's attention is aroused by persons or events in his environment. Edelman (1992), in *Bright Air, Brilliant Fire,* explained the relation between mind and brain, clarifying the relation between drive states and what we are able to admit to consciousness. Viewed from this drive model, the analyst listening to the patient hears what attracts the patient, what interests him, and how he seeks satisfaction in his world. When psychoanalysts ask why a particular behavior occurs, they are asking for motives or "causes" for the behaviors that lie within the patient. This interest in internal motives distinguishes psychoanalysis from other mental health fields; its contributions to understanding the causes of irrational behavior define the unique knowledge known as psychoanalysis.

Psychoanalysis is, once again, a rapidly growing field. Aggression is recognized as an important factor in shaping the psyche. Sexuality and aggression require outlets for an individual to successfully function. For the first time, violence can be understood in terms of when and why discharge mechanisms go awry.

Psychoanalysis as a model for reconstructing the "calamities of childhood" has been given up for a model that can be called the "here and now" approach. Cases that could never before be treated by psychoanalysis are now responding. We learned so much treating veterans in the fifties following World War II and in the seventies after Vietnam that many think of the shifts in analytic treatment as pre- and postwars. Yet, schisms remain. Some analysts focus attention on the transference of drives/impulses into the treatment, and others emphasize the analysis of defenses. Analysts discovered severe handicaps in reconstructing early experiences from current behavior and in analyzing resistances to the recovery of memories. When analysts, using the power of the positive transference, pressed patients to "tell all," patients tended to hide the truth from themselves in order to maintain positive feelings in the analytic relationship. If the patient recognized the truth, he was further blocked by a desire to be "respected" by the analyst. Revealing his hidden wishes humiliated or shamed him, caused guilt or left him castigating himself. Then there are those cases in which memories are manufactured to please the analyst who wants the patient to go in a particular direction. Even when these obstacles are avoided, verbalizing the hidden truths does not always bring an end to the pathology. Making the unconscious conscious does not cure!

The problem is that what is made conscious may be purely intellectual—the emotions are missing. They cannot be expressed in language.

Even such innovative analysts as Anna Freud, James Strachey, and Franz Alexander were unable to forsake the structural model. Strachey (1934) did emphasize the emotional immediacy of transference as the key to cure; however, he saw the inflexibility of character as a product of a strict superego, the implication being that character is the internalization of environmental values. For Alexander (1950), the work of analysis was to loosen the restrictions imposed by the superego. He suggested that the analyst function as an auxiliary superego, less rigid and demanding, with a lighter touch. In understanding transference, Strachey (1934) and others described the process of development of defenses in children. The child feels a strong impulse and feels compelled to act on it. If the action is experienced as dangerous, the child must find a way to manage it. If the child is overwhelmed by an oral sadistic wish, she can project it. In doing so, instead of fearing a loss of control of her own impulses, she fears a danger coming from outside herself. Using introjection, she reinternalizes the destructive image and holds it inside herself as an archaic object representation. This object representation then becomes a permanent part of her internal picture of what she believes that others are like. The introject then behaves as the child had originally feared behaving. It blames the child for lack of control of destructive impulses. It uses this destructiveness to attack the patient internally, to chastise, scold, and criticize her for traits unrelated to the oral sadism that started the whole process. This, for Strachey (1934), was the functioning superego. To further rid itself of this painful internal activity, the child can reproject onto a current external object this image of the rigid, dangerous introject, seeing important people in her life as having these characteristics. Externalizing the danger throughout her life, she can adopt the same orally aggressive impulses with which she started life. How, in this vicious circle, can psychoanalysis help?

Suppose that a patient comes to analysis stuck in infantile perceptions of himself and the environment and is living with archaic images, seeing the world around him as populated with dangerous objects. If he develops a transference to the analyst, will he not simply relive that same vicious circle in the treatment with the analyst?

An analyst may wonder how, when there is no language, he can work analytically with patients using such primitive defenses. If the patient forms a transference, won't the treatment simply duplicate the original archaic imagoes? Won't the transference work against a successful treatment?

The answer is no! But the course of treatment is complicated. If the patient can, in fact, direct urges into the transference relationship and the analyst can allow room for the expression of those urges in the treatment, then success is possible. First, the patient receives permission to make conscious some of his destructive impulses, including inappropriate sexual impulses. As the object of these impulses, the analyst needs the resiliency to tolerate the play of impulses in the interaction. The result of this first step is that the patient begins to separate both himself and the analyst from the archaic imagoes that haunt him. The work with the analyst at this level involves the use of the narcissistic transference and countertransference, more fully described in later chapters.

In 1949, Hyman Spotnitz, addressing the American Psychiatric Association, described his method for resolving these difficulties in treatment. Later, in the 1950s, his approach was described as modern psychoanalysis. Since that time, analysts trained in Spotnitz's (1969, 1985) techniques have used Freud's (1920) construct of innate destructiveness to understand how severe pathology is caused by the inability to process destructive impulses. The ability to read symbolic communications, the ability to hear what the body tries to tell us about its conflicts, the ability to understand fantasy and illusion are greatly enhanced when the role of Thanatos in emotional illnesses is recognized.

The beginning years of modern psychoanalysis were marked by successful treatment of schizophrenia, manic depressive disorders, and sociopathic patterns. Later modern psychoanalysis was applied to the treatment of addictions and somatic symptoms, including asthma, migraine headaches, and even life-threatening illnesses such as cancer and heart conditions.

In the pages that follow, I review basic theory and major modifications in the four decades following Freud's death. The section in this chapter on "Contemporary Developments" examines changes in psychoanalysis from Freud's death to the new millennium. The next chapter, "Messages from the It," explores how understanding drives leads to a deeper appreciation of the motivating forces behind thinking, feeling, and behaving, particularly in how we select the stage on which to play out our lives from what is available. The question I ask is whether drives can be user-friendly. Messages from the body are presented to illustrate how patients use their bodies as a language for describing their psyches. "The Language of Emotion," chapter 3, describes how an infant invents a psychic structure. It examines what is given biologically and what is learned. It is the story of how each person learns to use the world and compares how infants and emotionally ill adults work on drive satisfaction. It attempts to recapture the process by which the mind unfolds, a process perhaps not accessible to language. Included is a discussion of what the mind/emotional experience of the patient looks like during treatment.

Later, in chapter 4, "Creating Psychic Change," I consider how psychic change occurs in psychoanalysis. Case examples illustrate the process. This chapter covers changes in individual treatment and in group treatment. It opens with a discussion of how analysts begin the treatment.

In the concluding chapter, "Psychoanalysis in a Free Society," the institution of psychoanalysis is viewed as a tool in the creation of a free society.

Contemporary Developments

To understand the method of treatment used in psychoanalysis today, there is no better place to start than with the unconscious as described by Freud in 1915. Referring to the nucleus of the unconscious, he said that it contains impulses seeking discharge of their cathexes. He noted that various and even conflicting impulses, or pressures to act, exist side by side with no influence on one another, although they may combine to form an intermediate aim, that is, a compromise. Furthermore, the contents of the unconscious are timeless, neither altered by time nor having any reference to time, and uninfluenced by external reality. The activation of drives is determined solely by their relative strength. External reality has no influence.

Freud's (1915a) theory of unconscious process was based on understanding the mobility of energy and modes of discharge. Unbound energy with chaotic discharge was described as primary process. Through displacement, some outlet for repressed drives was provided, but only for a small portion of the cathexis seeking discharge. The rest remained connected to the unconscious idea and continued to seek discharge. The part that was allowed to enter into the preconscious operated in accordance with secondary process functioning in which energy is bound, organized in time, censored, and tested for reality. Connections were established to conscious memory, differing from unconscious ideas, which were only connected to memory traces.

Discharge can be achieved through somatic innervation, but this, too, can be blocked by the preconscious. As for the unconscious, it is helpless to discharge its cathexes (desire) on its own. The unconscious cannot bring about muscular acts without a connection to affects. It cannot connect an idea with the motor system. It is true that unconscious ideas continue to exist after repression as actual structures in the unconscious system, but they have been robbed of affect. As Freud (1915d) pointed out, all that is left in the unconscious of affects is a beginning structure that has been prevented from developing. Since affects, unlike ideas, are only processes for discharge, the main goal of repression is to inhibit the drive from being manifested in affects. These affects could be described as a type of sensation that presses for action.

Freud (1915a, 1915c, 1915d, 1920, 1923) separated the never-conscious, biological instinctual from the repressed unconscious. A split in the unconscious exists between biologically based inherited drives that operate on the discharge principle experienced as pleasure or displeasure, and the acquired repressed desire. The repressed unconscious is a response to the unconscious sexual aims of those who handle the infant's body. These messages from the adult to the child can only be received by the child when he is aware that he exists and when he is motivated to know how to relate to his environment. They are also rejected by the child and repressed into his own unconscious.

Because the unconscious cannot be perceived directly, existing as it does under the overlay of the preconscious, analysts have the opportunity only to peek into cases of regression and dreams. It was Freud's (1914b) theory that early experiences remain meaningless until development of self-awareness and sexuality permit a translation of experience.

As Freud (1915a, 1915d) portrayed it, repression does more than withhold ideas from consciousness; it prevents the development of affect and the startup of muscular activity. The conscious and unconscious continue to war for control of affects.

For repressed ideas, anxiety, a discharge mechanism, is an alternative to total suppression of affect. This mechanism operates in the service of the life drive. Often an affect is attached to a substitutive idea so that it can proceed from this substitute idea to action.

Freud (1914a) believed in discoverable truth and saw symptoms as distorted expressions of repressed ideas. The repressed unconscious, which does not talk, has its origins in early communications from the world. Lacan (1981) described the unconscious as like a language, in a world of words that creates a world of things. In empty speech, the word (signifier) is known, but what is signified is not. A modern analyst would say that affect is missing. To satisfy a desire, agreed-on speech with the internal other is required. Hidden discourse with the 'other' exists in symbols in which meaning is imprisoned. Life can be misconstrued in false connections by the conscious ego leading to functioning in a realm Lacan (1977) calls *the imaginary*. Lacan believed that the analyst must play in the arena of the imaginary to arrive at speech.

Lacan (1981) agreed with Freud (1920) that repetitions exist, but he raised the question, Repetitions of what? If a child becomes aware of himself when he looks into a mirror, it is only as a body. To become real to himself requires the presence of another. In a Lacanian analysis, the analyst serves as the 'other' who mirrors the patient (subject). Through that mirroring, the patient synthesizes his identity. Then the world is experienced through the interplay of self and other. Meaning is not conveyed through words but through the presence and the absence of the analyst (Other). In this process, the individual comes to exist and be named. The analyst's goal is to lead the patient to his true self, determined by the patient's drive destiny. However, the psychoanalyst must first process fantasy, delusion, and the false connections that sustain the analysand before any authenticity (true speech) can be achieved. Fantasies connected with the patient's desire are designed to solve such puzzles as "Where do babies come from?" "What is the difference between the sexes?" and "What does she (Other) want of me?"

Lacan (1981) noted that the sexually repressed unconscious originates in the unconscious desires and the discourse of the Other, from which questions of the subject's existence are articulated in the symbols of procreation and death. The questions are isolated as signifiers, not of his existence in the world but of his existence as a subject that extends to his "in the world" relation to objects.

How is Lacan used in today's psychoanalysis? We observe that when a patient suffers from a symptom, he searches for the meaning of that symptom. His conscious mind works to explain what he experiences. He arrives at superficial meanings that do not include the contents of the unconscious since these contents have been repressed and thus foreclosed. Because the patient does not want to know the truth of the unconscious, he remains in an analytic status quo, talking "as if" or, as Lacan (1977) would say, using "empty speech." To bring the patient to true speech, to give meaning to empty words, which is the patient's right, the analyst makes room in the treatment for the patient to have the freedom to desire. The analyst observes the patient's struggles to stay with superficial explanations to live in the repetition of the imaginary and to avoid his subjective nature, which brings with it knowledge of death. In true speech, the symbolic meaning of experience can be connected to the thing itself. We recognize that the full truth can never be known within the transference, yet the search for it can never be given up so long as one is breathing. During analysis, the analysand appears to organize life between desire and *jouissance*; that is, he tries to undo some loss and lack and to refind the "lost" primary object. What arouses his desire is the promise of fulfillment in fantasy, in the imaginary, not in reality. He seeks the internal experience of fulfillment.

Lacan (1977) saw the mirror stage as a time when the child can develop an ego designed to disavow desire. When the child in the mirror stage sees himself in the gaze of the Other, his future can be shaped by the recognition of lack. (I lack the breast, the penis.) Lacan (1977) says you may enter language only through recognition that you have both a mother and a father and that you cannot have union with the mother. This paternal metaphor, which he calls the "name of the father," cuts the bond to the mother, giving the child words to symbolize his loss.

Early contacts, according to Lacan (1981), are through the eyes. On all levels of drive, except the scopic, erotic desire exists when objects are seen as separate. Real connections wait to be changed into signifiers through the words of the Other. The Leforts' (1994) delightful report on a psychotic thirteen-and-a-half-month-old child living in an asylum for the temporary institutional care of infants during a mother's illness illuminates the above. Nadia had been separated from her mother at birth. Until her admission, she had been living in other hospitals and nurseries. At first, she had no mobility. She did not respond to adults. There was no object, milk, or breast. When fed, she lowered her eyes so as not to see the nurse, taking in nothing except satisfaction of bodily need. Nadia had crushed her real desire for the Other in order to satisfy her needs. One might say she operated on the level of biological survival (life/death) without a psychic life. Nadia had an emotional experience for the first time when glancing around her room; she saw other children being picked up by nurses. Envy (invidia) was aroused through scopic covetousness. Nadia entered the world of desire through longing. For longing to exist, an object must be seen as separate from the self. Nadia, by avoiding seeing the nurse when she ate, prevented separation and longing. There was a wish not to know the lack. She was able to exist in this way until she allowed herself to look around, which introduced to her the awareness of another. This occurred after a ten-month period of therapy. Before this, when sucking, she was *in* the other. To have a separate object either in the gaze or in the sucking required giving up the notion of oneness with breast and all other sources of pleasure. Earlier, part of the object had been glued to herself; then she experienced fascination, then a moment of moving out of fascination into a connection with another. Nadia was able to progress because she was not totally closed into fascination, which locks one onto the object. When the therapist called her by name, she responded with a turn of her head and a smile. Her hands clenched her caretaker's breast, and she said, "Mama." Her own name when spoken by the therapist became the signifier, and she never attached the image of the therapist to herself again. She learned the difficult lesson that the image was not she but belonged to the therapist, and the therapist became a witness to her loss although she still had a long way to go. The moment of that first loss was the moment in which she could be constituted as a self. Knowing that she was not the image that fascinated her, she learned that she was no longer the one who looks. At that very moment, entry into psychosis was possible. Children who cannot go beyond fascination with the image are precluded from awareness of the existence of the other. Instead, the Other remains an unbound signifier. For the child who can let go of fascination, this first image becomes the locus for all other signifiers, which begins the secondary process of what Lacan (1993) called *meshing*.

For Lacan (1993), the repression of the primary signifiers inaugurates the unconscious, thereby creating unconscious desire. Nadia in giving up her oneness with the other was able to enter the imaginary, in which she could seek to retrieve the lost object, the breast. In this way, she entered the symbolic order. Through love, in the form of a therapist who stayed with the goal of the therapy, Nadia found the *jouissance* of the real and pleasure in the body of the other. The passage from hallucination and fantasy to a realization of desire for the body of the other begins the life of the separate self.

In language, nothing is known of the real or imaginary since words relate to other words (signifiers relate to other signifiers), not to reality. They are symbols of desire.

In the imaginary, with significant others, one attempts to fulfill a desire, to fill a hole in the body, to complete the lack with the other. Before recognition of loss, fusion is attempted by means of the real body, more a sticking to than a joining.

In analytic work, Lacan's theories are particularly helpful when handling sexual repression. Freud (1915d) did not fully develop his understanding of how humans use words to create meaning. Lacan (1981) elaborated the role played by language, for which Freud laid the foundation by recognizing the distinction between word and the thing presentations and the importance of language in the acquisition of meaning. Freud found that words acquire meaning only by being linked to real experiences: visual, auditory, tactual, kinesthetic, and so forth. Words to be meaningful have to be linked to sensory impressions.

Outstanding among the works of the nineties is that of Laplanche (1999). He resurrected Freud's (1896) seduction theory in order to recognize the role of the unconscious wishes of the other as seduction and as a foundation for repression. He sees the Other as the source of an individual's sexual patterns and takes issue with the idea that the individual is the sole source of his unconscious fantasies. He argues, as Lacan (1977) does, for a decentering, an understanding of otherness as both an external other and internal other, a foreign body within, and the relation between them.

The postmoderns, like the moderns, have concluded that the search for memories of incest and abuse failed to demonstrate their significance. Abuse results in widely varying outcomes in the adult personality. When Freud (1906) grew suspicious of stories of seduction, he gave up seduction theory in favor of a theory of instincts and childhood fantasies. The poststructural analysts (Laplanche 1999) of this generation have suggested a return to a modified theory of seduction, in which the unconscious, if not the behavior, of the Other is crucial.

According to Laplanche (1999), early seductions are neither repressed nor available to the preconscious. They exist in limbo, unworked over and isolated, not resulting in symptoms until connected with sexuality through sexual arousal at puberty. It is with sexual development in the subject that the earlier event can become traumatic and institute repression. It is at the later moment that what Laplanche (1999) calls "translation" occurs. In Freud's (1895) case of Emma, her reaction when a shopkeeper touched her was disproportionate to the intensity of the experience. The memory of an earlier event that could not bring about a sexual response at that time was rearoused, and it was this arousal that led to Emma's anxiety. When sexual meaning is connected to the original experience, Laplanche (1999) finds confirmation in the fact that despite the shopkeeper laughing at her, she was pleased with him.

A careful reading of Freud (1893) shows that he believed it was the arousal of sexual feeling that set off hysterical repression. A memory may arouse an affect that was absent in the original experience but is available after puberty. It makes for a different understanding of what is remembered.

The erogenous zones, excitable breaks in body surface, are sites that can be stimulated by infants. This active behavior is independent of the presence of the object, in contrast to the satisfaction of certain oral drives when the breast is taken in from the outside.

Laplanche (1999) finds that the drive is neither a mystical entity, a biological force, or a concept on the frontier between the mental and the physical. It is the impact on consciousness by the repressed. The body is not the motor of the drive; the repressed acts on the body. Pressure comes from the demand for words to explain the untranslated repressed.

Laplanche (1999) also reworked Freud's (1920) opposition between life and death drives. He sees the death drive as leading to discharge of all tensions. Freud found the energy of the life drives represented in sexual desire. He found no corollary for the death drive but expected one would be discovered later.

With this in mind, the infantile experiences are viewed as neither sexual nor traumatic but simply meaningless events, pleasurable or unpleasurable, but without meaning. It is the intervention of a biological sexuality occurring at puberty that makes possible the interpretation of an experience as a sexually traumatic event. Early experiences are activated and given meaning *only* at a later date. They are neither created in early experience nor repeated in the experience with the analyst. They occur and are assigned meaning in the present depending on the awareness by the analyst of his own sexuality. In elaborating on Freud's (1896) early theory of seduction, Laplanche (1999) proposes a new role for infantile sexuality based on this concept of afterwardness and the primacy in the unconscious of the adult—in other words, what the Other laid down in personal prehistory. Contacts by the adult are enigmatic in that they are compromised by the unconscious wishes of the Other, wishes opaque to both the caretaker and the child. In this interpretation, events are seductive only because something enigmatic to the whole body and skin-ego is conveyed in washing, holding, talking, and other activities.

Laplanche (1999) includes verbal, nonverbal, and behavioral signifiers, which have unconscious sexual significance. Sexual communications from the unconscious of the caretaker can be taken in by the infant because of its openness to the actions and gestures of the surround. Some of the infant's earliest interpretations of experience are based on actions of the Other on the primitive body-ego or skin-ego of the infant.

In the handling of a child, sexual messages may be transmitted though not recognized by the adult. Laplanche (1999) refers to this as the primal seduction that results in the primal repression of the child. However, children's impressions are not actually repressed; they are consigned to a limbo in which no affect is attached to them. Because the childish impressions are not repressed, they can be thought of as untranslated, and this idea leads to an entirely different understanding of the repetition of infantile experience. One can no longer speak of repression of infantile experience. An event can only be repressed *when later it is translated*. When it surfaces in transference as sexual desire, *a desire, in the usual sense of sexuality, not present in the original experience*, it falls midway between seduction and fantasy.

Understanding Otherness
The modified version of seduction theory explains some of the communications of our patients around identification issues. Because affect was not connected with initial experiences, it could not be discharged but remained locked primarily in the body and its effects in the ego.

This probably is the single most important discovery of recent years: *Events of childhood are not repressed because they were* not *sexual or traumatic.* When unconscious mnemic traces of early experience are connected with sexual arousal, defenses come into operation: Phobias and anxiety may find a place in warding off the patient's understanding of experience.

Laplanche (1999) explains how the self comes into being in analysis within the translation model of repression. The unconscious of the Other that had eluded the child's early attempt to construct a world of relations is translated into a view on the messages coming in from adults and, in treatment, from the analyst. The repressed signifier is only a remnant of the message. Part of the message will have been translated, but part remains untranslated and in limbo. We cannot accept that all events not translated are in repression and thus committed to memory. Childhood events are inaccessible, although not repressed, so looking backward takes us only to early traces of conscious memories or to Freud's (1899) "screen memories." The search through memories does not include the repressed. The approach of psychoanalysis is an invitation to reunite the experiences with their appropriate affects in the transference in circumstances where sexual arousal is possible. In this, the split is healed.

Freud's (1910a) Leonardo da Vinci is an analysis, not of the unconscious, since Leonardo was not Freud's patient, but of a screen memory used in a search for an event corresponding to the vulture fantasy. It is not psychoanalysis because the affective meaning is missing.

The part of the message from the Other that is untranslatable functions outside consciousness as a source-object trying to reach consciousness. *Trieb*, or the drive for discharge, is seen in the desire for uniting affect with current experiences of sexual desire. Freud in 1920 emphasized life and death drives coming from primordial forces. In long-term analysis with psychotic patients, these conflicts play an important role and the search for sexuality a minor one. It was Lacan (1991b) and his followers who rediscovered the importance of the connection between the repressed desires and human sexuality.

For Freud (1916–1917d), the earlier moment took precedence over the later moment *Nachtraglichkeit*—deferred action stresses a progressive causality versus retrospective attribution. Material is subject at different times to rearrangement and retranscription. A failure of translation is reconceptualized by Laplanche (1999) as a fragmentation and dislocation of the enigmatic signifiers, the active production of a remainder that constitutes the unconscious as a separate mental system, a depositing of a residue or fallout from a translation process.

This challenge to the biological, or primary, unconscious, reaffirms the priority of the other in the seduction by the Other's unread messages and its later translation and repression in the formation of the unconscious.

Both Lacan (1977) and Laplanche (1999) see a drive not as an expression of endogenous needs but as the results of signifying relations between the subject and his other. They relegate the drives of self-preservation and the conflict between life and death forces to biology, reflexes, and the instincts. However, they note that the repressed leans on the biological id, the repository of needs.

The analyst is confronted with *trieb* from what is not translated, seeing that the distinction between life and death drives is behind the individual's conflict over sexuality. Lacan (1977) stated that every drive is virtually a death drive (i.e., to reduce tension) and that life and death refer to different aspects of the drive. Laplanche (1999) accepts Freud's (1923) ideas on tendency to fragmentation, unbinding, and discharge against a tendency to binding and synthesis.

The analyst's goal is to bring emotion into connection with buried ideas. The ultimate outcome brings the repressed and the never experienced to expression. In doing treatment, the analyst deals with the dissociated and with the unconscious that is alive both in derivatives and substitute satisfactions. The longings continue without cessation. Analysts have tended to begin with the derivatives that exist in the preconscious. Unfortunately these derivatives have the characteristics of the preconscious. Like the preconscious, they use secondary processes; they are certain, they are organized, and they are free from contradiction, unlike free-floating, primary processes of unconscious ideas. These derivatives are closer to consciousness and coexist with it until and unless their quantity reaches too intense a level. At that point, they break through as pathology.

Analysts need to think about the preconditions for the unconscious to acquire emotional language. Freud (1915d) thought that there must be censorship at each stage of development rather than a single censorship between preconscious and unconscious. He believed that a second censorship would be found between the preconscious and the conscious and that hearing (preconscious) and experience (conscious) are two different things. The repressed or disavowed cannot be reached by presenting the patient with information outside consciousness.

The idea that unconscious desire based on the desire of the Other opposes real drive satisfaction only occurred to analysts after Freud's death.

Lacan (1991a) in Book II of his seminars speaks of working through desire to drive satisfaction. Desire is seen as laid down by unconscious (repressed) messages from the Other and taken as law. The danger in analysis is that the analysand may unconsciously absorb the analyst's desire. This not only is a problem for ego analysts, who consciously work for adaptation and identification, but also may happen even when it is not the goal of the analyst.

Once Lacan separated drive and desire, he devalued desire and turned to the drive as leading to activity related to *jouissance* (Fink 1997). Lacan

(1977) emphasized that desire comes to a dead end; drives do not. From that point, he identified the true subject with drive, not desire. The authentic, or real person, became for Lacan a pursuer of satisfaction. Prior to analysis, he is kept down by the false ideals of ego and by superego restrictions.

Lacan's (1998) later work is dedicated to the aim of transforming the fantasy propped up by the desire that interferes with the pursuit of satisfaction. He concludes that the drive circles the demands of the object to a position where the urge to eat alternates with the impulse to be eaten, the urge to beat with the urge to be beaten. In this way, it maintains its contact with the language of the Other but in its newfound freedom seeks no approval of the Other. In analysis, the drive is finally freed to pursue its own goals within these limits.

For Lacan (1981), the patient in analysis is first dominated by the Other and then by the Other's desire, which has become the patient's desire as well. He finds his own reality in relation to the analyst.

According to Lacan (1977), the fully analyzed person, freed from the desire of the Other, is able to permit himself the satisfaction of his drives. Freud (1916–1917c) had described the neurotic as blocked in enjoyment, and later analysts took it as their function to reduce the stranglehold of the superego. In Lacan (1998), the symbolic restraint on drives is modified to the point where a person is free to seek drive satisfaction in her own way, neither compulsively nor inhibitedly, but with *jouissance*. The unconscious law of the Other called desire by Lacan (1977) is replaced by *jouissance*. Pathology keeps the subject stuck in the word and in the relationship between signifiers. Analysis puts the subject back in touch with emotion so that she can be an "enjoying subject."

Ego analysts who work with severe pathology have adopted the goal of further developing ego restraints in order to socialize the patient. Unlike the ego analysts, modern theorists have moved away from the aim of establishing "appropriate" behavior through transferential identification with the analyst and his personal values. When social adjustment is not the goal, the patient is more likely to present his drives. If the goal of analysis is to "traverse" the fantasy, one expects that satisfaction can only be reached through freeing the subject from the desire of the Other (superego) within the transference. If the analyst's goal is to free the patient for drive satisfaction and a connection with his own emotions, he must first cope with the patient's desire to remain within the fantasy of the Other. Patients when confronted with their own drives frequently reject them as disgusting or belonging to someone else. In strengthening the ego, the analyst attends to what the patient says he wants and to his rejection of his drives. The technique of interpretation of defense in ego analysis reflects the analyst's rejection of *jouissance*. Lacan (1977) used a technique he called *punctuation* to achieve the analyst's goal that the patient know his own emotions. When the patient presents a disguised drive, the analyst emphasizes the excitement hidden behind the defense to clear up any misunderstanding that the analyst may disapprove of the drive. The analyst tries to give the drive a place in the character, an acceptance that can allow further expression. The analysand is taught that he or she will come to exist separately from the analyst (the Other) when he accepts himself as a subject of enjoyment.

Between Freud's (1915a, 1919, 1924) work on masochism and Andre Green (1999) in *The Work of the Negative*, it is clear the role of victim should not be encouraged by the analysis. I treated a man who lost a younger brother to drug overdose and suffered during the following year from a pervasive sadness. I struggled to understand what fantasy blocked him from all other affects. Was there satisfaction in this painful affect? Did he want to see himself in this way? What really turns him on? I knew that he could pursue his satisfaction only if he knew what satisfaction was derived from his position as 'the one who suffers.'

Analyzing the defense before the drive confirms for the subject that he is being judged. With this sad man it was very difficult to bring him to pleasure in freedom from his brother, even though the sadness was also a defense against his sexual fantasies. So long as he was "getting off" on suffering, so long as he could not entertain the satisfaction of being free of this brother, so long as he maintained a fantasy of betrayal by a parent and by the analyst, he could not experience himself in his own sexuality. The relationship between his desire to be his mother's special boy and the torment in family life created by his brother's life-long illness continues to interfere or inhibit drive satisfaction. He lives in the fantasy and continues to doubt, rightly, that the analyst has the answers. He lives with the fantasy that "they did this to me," not that the choices and compromises were his.

As in all cases, the man's desire is to live in the fantasy, not in the satisfaction of drives. The new psychoanalysis is in agreement with Lacan's (1998) later view that in treatment desire can be freed from its equation with the object and distinguished from drive satisfaction.

Nobus (2000) has raised an interesting question on the goal of the analyst in the treatment of perversions. In his discussion of "A Child Is Being Beaten," Freud (1919) indicated that a perverse psychic structure requires an oedipal conflict. Lacan (1981) also noted the oedipal character of perversion stating that "[p]erversion does not appear as a pure and simple manifestation of a drive." To this he added that the neurotic mechanism of repression also exists in perversions in that perversion presents as a symptom, not as a manifestation of an unconscious drive. Lacan (Nobus 2000) finds that in a true perversion the accent is on the force of the object, whereas in neurosis the accent is on the desire of the Other. Freud (1893), Lacan (1981), and the moderns seem to have arrived at the same conclusion: that fantasy can be used to separate neurosis from perversion. Lacan (1981) says that in perversion the subject makes himself the object of the Other's *jouissance*, whereas the neurotic falsifies his own *jouissance*. If both pass through the oedipal, then both must deal with loss of enjoyment and the need to retrieve what was lost. Perverts differ from hysterics in that the latter try to arouse and sustain the desire of the Other. The hysteric's satisfaction comes from being desirable, not from the ability to experience enjoyment. The obsessional tries to neutralize the desire of the other and is satisfied by estrangement from the Other. Unlike the hysteric who wants to be desired, the obsessional does not. The pervert's discourse is on the right to *jouissance* (Nobus 2000).

The remarkable analogy between the pervert and the analyst is described by Nobus. The analyst's goal to restore the subject to his *jouissance* confronts us with the task of distinguishing how the analyst's desire is different from that of the pervert, who also maintains a right to *jouissance*. According to Freud (1916–1917c), regression to an infantile sexuality in perversion originates in repression of sexuality as in neuroses and unlike psychoses. The pervert suffers from the same anxiety over symbolic castration as the neurotic; however, his defense is disavowal. He is able to convince himself that the mother does have a penis (Nobus 2000). The pervert's unwillingness to accept the differences between the sexes results in the boy allowing himself only that *jouissance* that falls short of genital union. The mother unconsciously values the child because he can be used unconsciously to cover her symbolic lack of enjoyment and because she can obtain satisfaction in a carefree and selfish way with the child. The crisis for a child, according to Lacan (1993), lies in his discovery that being there is not enough. He must also fulfill the desire of the Other. The conflict for the child is whether to identify himself as the phallus for the mother and satisfy all her desires or to accept what Lacan (1977) calls the law of the father, relinquishing the relationship with the mother and agreeing to remain unsatisfied.

CHAPTER TWO

~

Messages from the It

Sex and Violence: Are Drives Friend or Foe?

Despite antagonisms and Freud bashing, psychoanalysis exerts enormous influence because of its knowledge of the dark side of human nature and its ability to plumb human depths. However, if human beings are as potentially destructive as psychoanalysis believes, can we learn through analysis to control these powerful urges? When we deny our nature, the results are illness, sadism, and war. The major difference between primitive and modern humans is not that we have become more peace loving but that we have acquired better tools for destruction. In studies of mass slaughter, we see the sense of power that comes from spilling blood. Theories of superiority like Naziism exist because they allow humans to project their dark side onto others.

Psychoanalysts have become increasingly aware that libido theory alone does not explain fully what is observed when we treat patients. It does not make sense of sadism or masochism, of perversions, murder, or suicide. It was not until Freud (1924) studied masochism that he learned that the amount of suffering one is willing to endure is in the service of object protection. It was then that he understood the need of destructive urges to find expression. The earlier belief that frustration of pleasure was a sufficient explanation of destructive behavior could not account for the repetition of unpleasure under certain circumstances. When Freud (1920) posed a theory of destructive as well as constructive drives, he realized that psychoanalysis would have to be reformulated in terms of understanding the aggressive drive as separate from the libidinal drive. Freud was aware that patients repeated irrational behavior, but it was not until late in his career that the concept of a repetition compulsion and its connection to a death drive was formulated. Eventually he concluded that to avert war and destruction, society must encourage attachments to 'anything' that fosters Eros.

At present analysts are concerned with thoughts about how patients learn to deal with innate destructive impulses. I had a patient say to me, "My final act will be to destroy the shell that houses me." Analysts study how their patients use Eros and Thanatos to process the destructive aims of their personalities.

When people come to treatment, they may be coping with pathological fusions or purely destructive drive states. I have a patient who can't have an erection. He also can't stand to be fondled. Sex frightens him because of its destructive connotations. His solution, prior to analysis, was to isolate himself and "keep busy." I treated another man, Michael, who was unhappily married for thirty-five years. He could not leave his wife. They had sexual relations but barely spoke to one another. He was sexually involved with another woman for whom he had positive feelings. He said, "She is intelligent, sensitive, outgoing and loves me. Time with her is pure pleasure." He has a body symptom for which no doctor has made a diagnosis: all-over body itch. The woman who loves him comforts him. The itch subsides when he is with her. It returns when he sleeps with his wife. This man does not say that he hates his wife, but he remains with her and feels tortured. He is torn between pleasure and unpleasure. His wife cannot work because of illness. His children torment him. Home life is a torment. The revelation that led to understanding this patient was his complaint that he is indifferent to sex. His mistress arouses infantile longings, particularly the longing to be held. His fantasy is that she will take care of him in his old age. He has sexual contact with her for her sake. This, and the recognition that he needs the storms of family life, led to the recognition that in his fantasy life, he directs destructive longings to the family and his desires to be nurtured by the perfect mother to his mistress. Life and death forces struggle against each other. Neither of these patients is able to fuse life and death drives.

No flight is available for them or for us from instincts because instincts come from internal sources and must find a playing field in which to express themselves. They exert a constant force. We see with these two patients the suffering connected with conflicting impulses and particularly when splitting permits the separation to stress different feelings for different objects instead of the normal ability to love and hate the same objects.

Freud (1937a) learned that making the unconscious conscious did not always lead to the amelioration of symptoms. He described the compulsion to repeat as the patient's way of remembering what he could not find language to express (Freud 1914c). Analysts, therefore, turned their attention from recapturing repressed memories to a reliving of conflicts within the analytic relationship. The transference became the playground in which the patient had freedom to display everything in the way of instinct arousal and pathogenic repetition.

With the emphasis on transference, analysts had to decide when and what to interpret. Since it was clear that patients act outside their own awareness—that is, their functioning is a result of unconscious motives—the question asked was, "How can we study motives if the patient cannot tell us about them?" Analysts were coming to the belief that each patient could be expected to bring his or her conflicts into the treatment directed toward the person of the analyst. However, analysts were not yet agreed on whether the analyst should only offer transference interpretations, or might they include interpretations of the patient's external life?

Freud (1912a) and followers of Melanie Klein (1946) emphasized the transference in which motivating drives entered the analytic scene because they possess a permanent urge to discharge. Since the analyst is available as a transference object, these urges can be expected to seek an outlet in the analysis. This view of transference as the central fact of analysis brought with it a recognition that the real character of the analyst might interfere with the way the patient needed to view the analyst in order to work through his conflicts. One of the discoveries that led to further discourse among practitioners was the fact that what is transferred to the analyst occurs through a process called *displacement* or, in earlier fixations, through a process called *projection*.

If the transference was to be the central concern of the analyst, it was to be expected that treatment would focus on the appearance of drive states directed toward the analyst and defenses against their appearance. The publication of "The Ego and the Id" (Freud 1923) led to a further theoretical split between analysts. Did the analyst want to bring affects (emotions) connected with the drives into the room, or did he want to analyze only the defense structure of the ego in the belief that the patient could be cured through the interpretation of his defenses without delving deeply into "live" impulses focused on the analyst? For those concerned with bringing the drives to life in the analytic relationship, a further question was whether frustration of drives, as Ferenczi (1924) suggested, was needed.

While other analysts trained by Freud and his colleagues were studying genetic development and seeking rules that would help them to sequence their interpretations according to the patient's level of maturation, Theodor Reik, who had relocated to New York City, introduced a new concept that he called *surprise*. He believed that regardless of how an analyst tries to structure the treatment, most discoveries come from the analyst's intuitive ability to be in touch with the patient's unconscious. This way of relating "unconscious to unconscious" can uncover repetitions that the analyst's conscious mind has not yet conceived of.

The entrance of modern psychoanalysis on the analytic scene occurred at a time when the expression of destruction and aggression had increased recognition. Although there had been sufficient evidence in history of the role of aggression in human interactions, World War II seemed to awaken us to the role of the aggressive instinct in human development. People who are meaningful to us are objects of all of our feelings. Once we know that aggression is inborn, not a product of environment, we want to know how innate aggression can be influenced. The theories that were used during the thirties and forties no longer seemed relevant. For instance, Franz Alexander (1950) focused on the analyst's task of modifying a severe superego that led to rigid, inhibited personalities. Ego analysts, who emphasized undoing pathological defenses, and the analysts who emphasized relating to patients intuitively, "unconscious to unconscious," were no longer in vogue. With the modern approach, the environment seemed to provide the stimulus for satisfaction seeking. Frustration remained a cause for aggression but not the only cause, and usually not sufficient provocation for the amount of aggression unleashed. More often, rationalizations were created to justify destructive actions. Before the moderns, Melanie Klein (1946) and Anna Freud (1949) debated whether the mix of Eros and Thanatos was a cause of conflict and a basis for pathology. Klein believed that in loving, as soon as the person is recognized as separate, one will be afraid of innate impulses to attack the loved object. She observed that guilt resulted from destructive impulses experienced for those who are needed or 'loved'. Anna Freud (1949, 1953) disagreed. It was her belief that opposing instincts exist side by side in childhood without producing conflict. Modern analysts decided they were both right. If opposing impulses could be fused, then there would be no conflict, and some are. Small children test the waters when they say, "I hate you." Children under a year may say, "No," and slap the back of their hands when one part objects to an impulse in the other. However, these children may be involved in object pleasing and concerned with whether an adult approves of them. More research will be needed to determine whether an infant, prior to awareness of the Other, can object to his own impulses. We can observe clinically that at some points one's own impulses are experienced as dangerous and generate anxiety.

Why We Repeat

It has been shown that in the presence of stimulation, either from internal needs or from the environment, individuals want to respond. Higher mental processes do not play a significant role in the response to a hot poker. Other urges for relief that one cannot satisfy oneself lead to seeking others for satisfaction. Successful living requires that we become aware of others, use our experiences, and develop some tolerance of frustration in the search for satisfaction. In the transference our patients demonstrate that they learned they could not survive without another person to care for them. For a time they defend against conscious recognition of this wish. Eventually the analyst becomes the only person who can fill the role. The analyst acquires value if she helps to reduce tension or helps a patient to cope.

We know that drives or instincts do not appear in pure form. The desire for satisfaction requires assertiveness and seeking behavior. Freud (1930) believed that humans struggle against all odds to live simply because they are alive and want to continue. It appears that consciousness also craves continuity. Descartes once said, "A grain of sand in a sea of sand stands up and says, 'I exist.'"

Anna Freud (1936a) made a major contribution to modern analytic thinking when she recognized that the fundamental rule of psychoanalysis, to free associate, could lead to negative therapeutic reactions in some cases and to monotonous repetitions in others. As a result of her experiences with patients, she recommended a relaxation of the command given to patients to free associate.

One can withdraw from events in the external world by taking flight; however, drives have an unfriendly aspect in that no flight from them is possible. Our drives are inside us and cannot be shaken off. The aim of these drives is to reduce tension through discharge. Of course, sometimes increases in tension states are desirable, too, because they lead to pleasure. As we mature, we turn to the external world for instinctual gratification. "We are born to die, but interrupted by love."

It is difficult to accept the idea of a death instinct or to understand a wish to return to nonexistence, yet science confirms that living matter does seek lower and lower tension levels. Evidence from long-term analyses verifies a continuing conflict between the wish to be, to continue life and its strivings, and the wish not to be, to end the struggles. "To be or not to be, that is the question." Since we do not experience our own or our patient's instincts directly, we can only infer the existence of life and death drives. Analysis of both the patient's and our own defenses against particular ideas and affects are the clue. We can think of ego defenses as attempts to weaken the power of life and death urges by robbing ideas of their affects. In hysteria one renders ideas harmless by transforming them into somatic symptoms. A conversion may appear as a motor enervation or as a hallucinatory sensation. Obsessional illnesses block the connection between affect and ideas by compartmentalizing them so they lose their links to each other. The affects may become attached to conscious ideas about which the person finds himself obsessing without rhyme or reason.

Freud (1915c) observed that when a hostile or loving thought gives rise to distressing emotion, the person may put aside the thought, but it reappears in a displaced form. The analyst is then impressed by the incomprehensible strength of the resulting obsession. Sadistic, masochistic, voyeuristic, exhibitionistic, or homosexual preoccupations may become separate from conscious sexual longings. The phobic person simply avoids those situations that will arouse undesirable feelings. For example, in Freud's (1905a) case of unrequited love, the anxiety that would have been aroused by drive was prevented by avoiding those situations that would arouse anxiety. The life drive leads individuals to do anything to stay alive. They will assimilate, accommodate, or make structural internal changes to preserve life. Such accommodations require the person to combine assertive aggression with the pleasure seeking. Drives seeking discharge may use reversal, displacement, or sublimation. By changing the object of the drive, one can turn the impulse against the self. In narcissism, self is substituted for an external object. We think of masochism as sadism turned back on the patient's own ego.

A patient whose parents tortured her, in turn, tortured her younger brothers and sisters, avoiding the narcissistic or passive experience of self-torture as is seen in depressive patients. In childhood, activity increases as the child becomes more aware of the outside world. In regression we see this process in reverse. The patient returns to earlier stages and passive aims. We frequently observe a reversion to the passive position. In narcissism when the person gives up loving and longing in favor of being loved, he reverts from activity to passivity. A patient moving from the passive to the active position complains that he doesn't have enough feelings. He wants to care more about others. He worries about his indifference to the world and to people around him. The narcissist, on the other hand, complains, "Nobody loves me; I'm not loved. What did I do wrong? What is wrong with me?" or, "The world is a terrible place, all bastards. They can't appreciate a person like me."

I have a patient who is always thinking about the right place for his next vacation. This man has a wonderful job. He is known to be brilliant, does fine work, but he never thinks of his work as enjoyable. He only obsesses about the next vacation, although recently he told me he plans to retire soon and live in a wonderful climate. Since he really does not enjoy leisure—it makes him restless—his future looks dim if he follows his fantasy. He was trained early in life that work is work and play is play.

When analysts think about the unconscious and its effects on the emotional experiences of their patients, they divide those parts of the unconscious that are archaic, constitutional factors from the layers built up through experience because they had to be eliminated from consciousness when unpleasure got connected with them. As we study our patients, we learn that each level carries with it a different kind of thinking. Does teething arouse sadistic impulses toward the breast? If the mother did not pull away when bitten, would one, nevertheless, develop envy, want to incorporate the breast, and want to destroy it? Does the sense of self and of inadequacy at not having total control of the breast have more to do with the sadistic attitudes that unfold in infants? Children at the anal stage demonstrate their wishes to hurt and destroy in addition to anal erotic impulses. Phallic children appear totally inconsiderate of the feelings of others. As they satisfy their need to exhibit and view, they remain unaware of the effect they have on others. They wish others out of their way and are particularly hostile to rivals or competitors.

How Are Drives Friends?
Freud (1920) connected the death drive with both the wish to reduce tension and with aggression. In "Outline of Psychoanalysis," he (1940) described how fusion of sex and aggression was required for successful sexual intercourse. As analysts tried to clarify the meaning of dual drive theory, they had to face facts: Clinical experience did not bear out the equating of the death drive with aggression. All we can see when with patients are tendencies to move between tension increase and tension decrease. Although Sternbach (1975) connected aggression with the life drive, he observed that in the sexual act both arousal and diminution of tension occurred. Patients tend to develop characterological patterns of rhythms, and he noted, this buildup (life) and reduction (death) are two elementary demands placed on mental life. According to Sternbach, coitus is a rhythmic approach and avoidance of two bodies, each engaged in the rise and fall of tension and stimulation through this contact. Buildup leads to the same pain that all life actions lead to. If the act did not lead to retreat and return to buildup, we

might expect death before climax. Throwing oneself into life, or tension buildup, a leap alternates with a decrease in tension in an overall pattern of larger increases fluctuating rhythmically with smaller decreases to total discharge after the excitement reaches its climax. Pleasure can be seen as anticipated discharge accompanied by the excitement of the buildup.

Spotnitz (1976) in 1969 had already written about the tension buildup and release as a feature of what occurs between analyst and analysand. Both he and Sternbach understood sexuality as self-preservation and destructiveness, as fusions and defusions of Eros and Thanatos, tension buildup and discharge.

Setting tension reduction in opposition to the sexual instinct does not cover these facts. The two sets of instincts war in pathology but work cooperatively in living acts such as intercourse. Earlier theories posed the death drive as a passive force. We now can see it as an energy exerted to create the act of tension reduction. When seen merely as a passive force, it was possible to discard dual drive theory, viewing tension reduction as the downside of arousal.

Presuming that sex and other living acts are a combination of Eros and Thanatos, tension buildup and tension release, then what we see clinically can be better understood as various balances of rhythm combining both forces, neither one existing alone. In the analytic literature, libido still carries the old meaning of sexuality alone, rather than the fusion of opposite tendencies. Freud (1920) himself posed love and hate as opposites. Hate is usually reserved for those we love. Those who are not recipients of our love do not deserve our hate. In a later chapter I will discuss prejudice, which is a pathological process of splitting love and hate. This can be understood as a failure of the psyche to fuse the drives, a breakdown.

When we think of the struggle each of us engages in to experience satisfaction, we find that it is only through the struggle that maturation is possible. Infants have to learn first "what is me" and "what is not me." There is a gradual development of functions that lead to drive satisfaction at each stage in development. One of the characteristics of the mature person, we have found, is that drives from the various levels have not simply disappeared with maturity but have found satisfactory, or more satisfactory, outlets in life-enhancing activities.

Using coitus as a model of life, it is clear that the greatest satisfaction is ultimately achieved in total discharge. Life is pleasurable in the expectation of greater levels of discharge. Life is also feared in the unconscious recognition of the death instinct as an important ingredient in living. Orgasm is only possible if opposing tendencies can be fused to serve one aim. This idea was an important theoretical shift (Sternbach 1975) from previous writings on the death instinct, which spoke at large of the struggle between Eros and Thanatos, with Thanatos viewed as the destructive goal. Over the history of psychoanalysis, most writers who rejected a death instinct did so because they identified this set of instincts with innate destructiveness. If we view life as a detour on the road to death with two tendencies in the body, we are then free to study the circumstances under which destructiveness and violence make their appearance. Modern analysts have emphasized the quantitative factor in the inability to fuse drives. A quantitative overload for which the individual can find no immediate outlet for discharge does lead to a bottled-up condition. Pathogenic blocks, somatization, and bottled-up, flooded conditions result. A pathological solution that is life preserving is detachment or withdrawal, defenses usually considered serious illnesses. Lacking such defenses, individuals may have no alternative but to turn to destructive actions for release. Earlier in modern analytic technique, practitioners mistakenly thought that discharge of rage and hostility might cure the patient who was on overload. Many were surprised to learn that when much analytic time was devoted to such discharge, the patient merely developed a preference for explosiveness but continued to be bottled up. One of the dangers was that satisfaction of vindictive fantasies eliminated the motivation for change. Modern analysts developed other approaches to this condition, and these led to a less stimulating analytic environment, one geared to the tolerance level of the patient. Modern analysts were learning by experience that destructiveness is not necessarily what requires discharge. An outlet for tension can allow for an abatement of destructiveness. Intuition is required to determine the balance between rageful statements to the analyst, lowered tension levels in the treatment, and aids to establishing a narcissistic identification of the patient with the analyst. A paranoid schizophrenic patient, afraid of harming people he was close to, improved when he became an avid bowler.

Tension release appropriate to the drive level on which there is an active conflict is the solution in the analytic working through. Finding the appropriate form of discharge follows Brenner's (1982) recommendation of substituting a healthier discharge for a pathological one. In a study of the most successful styles of analysts with patients, I have observed that being the enemy does not work. Analysts who do not criticize the patient, tell him about his pathological behaviors, or get the patient to attack the analyst appear to the patient to be on his team. When it is necessary to confront a patient with a piece of his own behavior, an angry analyst does not have a positive effect. It doesn't help to attack the patient's objects; he seems able to do a good enough job of that. I heard of one analyst who had been identified in the patient's mind with a torturer. One day he showed up unannounced at the analyst's office and shot him point blank while stating, "I have to get you out of my head." He couldn't shake off the preoccupation with what he believed were the analyst's thoughts about him. Unfortunately, the shooting did not change anything for the patient. Dead, wounded, or alive, the fantasy analyst continued to occupy his thoughts.

When the Body Speaks, Can We Hear It?

The Mind–Body Relation

The mind is charged with the responsibility to process messages, normal and pathological, from all body parts, sending and receiving information and directing actions. As a result, emotional tension can originate in the body. Simple examples of physiological overload resulting in stress are swimming in cold water, sitting for prolonged periods at a computer, and losing sleep. Conversely, emotional tensions may influence body processes. Preparing for a final exam can result in stomach distress, headaches, rashes, and so forth. Research confirming the connection between mind and body is available in the psychosomatic literature on hypertension, peptic ulcers, chronic bowel conditions, asthma, and other respiratory illnesses.

Freud (1905b) likened psychic function to all other bodily processes, basing his theory of mental functioning on, first, the satisfaction of instinctual drives and the defenses against their discharge and, second, the defenses against external stimulation. He learned clinically that somatic conditions develop when there are no other satisfactory methods available for the discharge of internal stimulation. On the other hand, it was Freud's (1926) belief that when the individual lacks sufficient defenses against external stimulation, psychosis may follow. This interaction between emotions and the body has concerned analysts because of the dangers when erotic feelings or destructive feelings are turned inward to create body symptoms.

To the practicing analyst, the body and the mind reflect different ways of expressing human conflict. Each patient must be studied to determine the particular way in which he or she expresses conflict and, specifically, how the body is involved in the expression of emotional conflict. When talking about regressed patients, analysts often use the language of the physiologist to describe psychic processes. They speak of impulses, of their discharge, of bottled-up energy, and of resistances to discharge. Psychoanalysis was, after all, born out of biology. Analysts have never denied the significance of biological processes to their understanding of their patients. In some cases the patient supplies concrete evidence of the connection between mind and body. Patients sometimes provide us with clues to their inner struggles through expressive enervation such as blushing, weeping, hysterical laughing, headaches, allergies, back pain, and numerous other symptoms of stress. When, for example, a patient weeps repetitively in his sessions, we are witness to a mind–body interaction. The body becomes the patient's way of communicating with the analyst. It is not different from the patient who tells us a dream. Dreams may be presented by the patient to inform the analyst of something going on in his emotional life, something he cannot report directly in adult language. So, too, are body symptoms. For some time analysts tried to link specific bodily illnesses with specific emotional conflicts. Since Freud (1914a) successfully linked oedipal wishes to hysterical paralysis and other conversions, it was hoped that all somatic conditions could be thus understood.

As psychoanalysis evolved as a method of treatment, it broadened its interest in physical illnesses. When Freud (1909a, 1916–1917a) worked with oedipal character problems, he assumed the existence of unresolved emotional conflicts originating in the family romance. He was aware also of preverbal difficulties in the personality from oral and anal conflicts. It was an important shift in the psychoanalytic treatment method when modern day analysts included preoedipal conflicts within their analytic work, a shift that led analysts to consider bodily symptoms as manifestations of preverbal longings. At early phases in the process of maturation, the child is unable to reduce the stress of conflicts through mental functioning. Unresolved emotional conflict means that there has been inadequate discharge of bottled-up energy. What motor pathway an individual chooses at this stage depends on her individual history. A person who resorts to somatic discharge repetitively has established physical pathways for tension reduction originating in the very earliest period of her life. If a person is stuck at this method of tension reduction, she has laid the groundwork for serious physical illnesses.

Those diseases that have been found to be connected with symptoms of the voluntary system—that is, with the perceptual and neuromuscular functions—seem to be related to the inhibition of destructive impulsiveness. Physiological preparation for action, later inhibited, can be expected to cause changes in metabolism and circulation (e.g., hypertension). Neuromuscular preparation for fight accompanied by muscular inhibition may result in a corollary physiological response (e.g., arthritis).

Patients in early regressed states may communicate their nuclear conflicts through reports to the analyst of physiological reactions. Behind these communications, the analyst may discover a hidden question: "Do you care about me?" "Am I a loving person?" "Can I tolerate intimacy?" "Am I afraid you will annihilate me, that I will annihilate you?" "Will you overwhelm me, destroy my sense of who I am?" And so on. Analysts have been doing better at reading the hidden meanings behind somatic symptoms because they have learned that these are the language of preverbal or very early infantile conflicts.

A case demonstrating a connection between allergies and emotional life came to my attention. The patient, on entering the treatment room, said, "I cannot lie down because of my allergy. And my head is throbbing. May I sit up and not look at you?" I asked about his allergy, and he responded, "I just walked over across the park, and it was full of pollen. Can we have the air on?" he asked. "The open window lets the pollen in. May is the worst month." He sat in a chair and reported problems with sex and his wife. He added that there are women from whom he wants affection and the kind you want Saturday night date sex with. He confides that he has trouble integrating the two. He feels nausea. I get the message that he is having negative feelings that he objects to because they interfere with affectionate feelings. I wait and he continues. While he was walking through the park, he had a silent argument with me about my raising my fee. Then he thought about the pressure he is under to pay bills. He described himself as a workhorse. That reminded him that it is the anniversary of his mother's death. He said there were further thoughts as he walked over: His wife was not considerate of him; he might lose me. Either he must give me every cent he earns or not be able to see me. His head is still throbbing. I say, "May is a cruel month. Walking through the park arouses longings and fears." He says, "Neither you nor my supervisor care anything about me. I am just one of the mob that comes to your offices." He appears distraught and agitated. After some exploration, he asks me how I feel about what he is saying, and I say, "I like working with you. If you cannot afford the fee, perhaps I should send you a patient who can pay as much as you pay me." With that, the patient began to cry. He says that his head, which he is holding, is beginning to. . . . He pauses and then says, "It is like when I take a decongestant."

At the next session the patient connected some of the unexpressed feeling with his asthma. He felt he should have gone to the couch, not sat up. It would have been easier than looking at me. "Even though I lowered my eyes, I kept getting sick. . . . When you said you liked working with me, I felt you cared, but then I had to face that feeling. You care for me! What is my problem with intimacy? Just thinking about it interferes with my breathing. And when I make love, I get out of breath. My wife notices it because I involuntarily hold my breath. When I feel intimacy building, I feel endangered, in a sense overpowered. It is clear to me I am someone who has lived life not expecting much love. I work hard, get depleted, then get angry because I am not getting much. It's hard to live life without an exchange of love. Me, I have lived for praise. Other people use sex as pleasure, as nourishment. For me, it is a source of anxiety. Even getting a woman into bed is an active thing, not a letting go. When I was nine or ten, my mother wanted me to protect her so she took me into bed with her. I just lay there in a wooden way."

With cancer patients, one finds similar coping mechanisms. Many possible causes have been documented in the literature; for example, an emotional loss is frequent prior to the onset of cancer. So, too, is a physical trauma. Preceding leukemia, researchers found a high incidence of flu and pneumonia. We know trauma can reduce the effectiveness of the body's immune system, thus establishing a readiness for cancer. In the analysis of cancer victims, the difficulty is in reversing the patient's tendency to discharge tension in life-destructive ways. The problem is that despite the patient's and the analyst's best intentions, the patient cannot say everything. Freud (1912a, 1913) discovered that resistance invariably set in. When a patient is told to say everything, he finds he is blocked. A more serious limitation is that saying everything, without a connection to an object, is fruitless. Because the emotional connection is missing, the analyst must actually go through the stages of maturation with the patient. In sessions, the patient talks until he reaches a block. The analyst silently analyzes the block. The block will come up repetitively in the sessions until, through the relationship to the analyst, the resistance can be resolved. Analysts do not work by magic. Usually they help the patient to tell them what is necessary for the patient to move on from the point at which he is stuck. As language is integrated with needed affects, the ego expands. Eventually each patient experiences the relationship with his analyst as 'new'. Negative self-attitudes as well as parental mishandling can be reversed only by the analyst's patience and interest in his patient. Working with cancer patients has the further difficulty that the cancer is fast growing, so the treatment must be conceptualized as short term. Can we ask transference to unfold at a pace that will save the patient? Analysts have found that they must be more active, a different kind of object for the patient, because if a lengthy negative transference were to be permitted, the patient might die before change could occur.

In some cases, an analyst may not even want to attempt analytic work. I had one patient who came in with a metastasized brain cancer and the belief that she should try everything on the off-chance that something might work. She was receiving chemotherapy concurrently with the analysis. In addition, she was encouraged to change her eating habits, which she did. This patient's

personality fit perfectly the cancer personality profile: She was extremely po-
lite but when she spoke revealed a great deal of repressed rage. When she
learned that the cancer had been reversed, she left treatment. She did not
want a treatment that would involve introspection, particularly regarding
her inability to be close with others. She left without knowing what had
caused the remission. Was it chemotherapy, analytic session, a change in
diet, or some combination? She had not been in touch with her rage; the
treatment did not touch it. The point at which she left was the point at
which she had her first reason to be angry with me. She had asked that I take
a particular action that would demonstrate to her that I cared about her.
Rather than do it herself, she wanted me to actively intervene in her affairs.
For two months as she tried to convince me, she debated whether or not to
leave. As she got better, she got closer to her rage, but she could not discuss
it with me. In my presence she felt it would be undignified, even though she
could discuss it with her husband. She told him, "She's not interested in taking care of me!"

A woman consulted me whose background was in research. Her work life
had concentrated on conventional research questions such as, "Should students live in mixed dorms?" Her department would send out questionnaires
to five thousand students, collate findings, and run statistical tests to back up
their conclusions. She talked about how boring this work had been. She
wanted to study mother–child relationships and other women's problems.
She had made substantial financial contributions to her college, so as she got
stronger she asked to design research projects at home to be carried out by
the staff under the aegis of the university. She oriented her projects to ideas
that would help the university to plan student life. Her physical strength and
interest in this work seemed to increase as she planned and talked about
what she wanted. We had enjoyable sessions based on her enthusiasm for the
future. The transference from the beginning was positive. We never dealt
with the negative experiences of her life or negative feelings in the analysis,
only in making life more interesting. This was, of course, an unusual analytic
stance. She said she had never had a relationship like this. Everyone enraged
her except me. It was my belief that because of her cancer, we did not have
time for a negative transference to be worked through. While the rage was
never brought into the transference directly, it was worked on in the sense
that we tried to alleviate some of the external conditions that created her
rage (i.e., job dissatisfaction). Her son had tended to avoid her because of his
desire 'not to know' but as her motivation increased to have a more pleasing
life, she arranged holidays so that he could bring his friends to ski resorts and
Caribbean vacations. She had bad feelings while she learned how to relate

constructively to her son and his friends. She had always been a critical mother; learning to create pleasure in the relationship helped to swing the emotional balance from totally negative to pleasure in living.

To explain this treatment, I examined what I thought were the secondary gains in the sessions, a freeing up of her fantasy life. I knew that resistance to fantasy was a problem common to cancer patients who seem reality oriented. This is a resistance that has roots in the first few months of life. A newborn baby fixes his eyes and begins to see things. This focusing process brings about constitutional and physical development. The ability to take in visual images precedes the development of fantasy life. An infant must first see the breast in order to have a fantasy about it when it is missing. The failure to focus leaves the infant blank inside, but not quite; tuning out is replaced by the experience of an internal roaring, a churning unconnected with outside images. Probably the most adaptive trait at this stage of growth is the ability to look out. I believed that that was what she and I worked on in her sessions.

I learned early in my career that one can't remove the resistance to fantasy by telling a patient to fantasize. When I began my practice in the 1950s, I innocently approached a VA hospital referral, diagnosed as paranoid schizophrenic, with pressure to produce a fantasy. He walked into my office blown up with intense rage and suspicion. I learned, quite by accident, that he could not close his eyes and visualize anything, so I gave him exercises. I told him to look at my desk, close his eyes, and tell me what he saw. He became agitated and suspicious of my motives. Rather than overcoming a problem, it pointed out his deficiency, resulting in increased anger.

When a patient can allow for mutual fantasy with the analyst, the relationship can come to have special emotional significance. With another patient, the analytic sessions were the first occasion when she could enjoy a fantasy. When she first came to my office, she had cancer. She had consulted a number of analysts, finding out from friends who was the biggest name in the field, but never had a satisfying experience. They told her many things about herself, but she always left dissatisfied because she believed she could have arrived at their ideas on her own. She had one session with me and announced that she would like to come back sometime, but she was on her way for major surgery. Following the surgery, she asked to begin treatment. She had been involved for years in court battles with her husband. Most of her energy went into fighting him. When he disappeared, the helplessness proved too much for her. Her personal fortune had been dissipated in international court battles. She came to me because she wanted to stop the spread of the cancer, and she was convinced only talking could do it. She was the child of withdrawn parents who had no interest in what was on her mind as a child. Weekly contacts were enough to help stabilize her moods. My understanding of what helped in the treatment was the reversal of the original situation in which talking was not encouraged. The transference was not just verbalized, but lived. She liked talking to me and felt that I enjoyed what she had to say. I did enjoy the sessions because everything she talked about was a fantasy. I had several fears, however. Frequently, I thought that I was getting too much gratification, and this caused misgivings. Another fear was that she might stop having fantasies, that disappointment and depression might leave her with no other resource for fighting for life.

Understanding my fears with this woman led me to articulate some of the major countertransference issues in work with cancer patients. Since we were not engaged in standard psychoanalytic practice, I worried about whether this was the "right kind of treatment for her." I was doing nothing to "analyze" the emotions that were implicated in the cancer. This feeling of uncertainty about my work is a feeling easily induced with cancer patients. The feeling was of traveling uncharted territories, never sure what was right. The stakes were enormous, dealing with life and death in an immediate way.

Another, less rational fear was of contracting the patient's disease. It has been documented that cancer is not infectious and not transmitted through biological contagion, but the fear persisted. Eventually I connected the idea of contagion to its historical roots in the mother–child relationship. Analysts had done significant research on the transmission of feelings and intentions, both voluntarily through words and gestures, and involuntarily. Escalona (1963) wrote on emotional contagion, a process in which a feeling state transmits itself from baby to mother, to explain how mothers and babies get psychologically attuned, a necessary condition for growth. This notion of emotional contagion has had a major influence on how to think about cures. Both analyst and patient are affected by the emotional states of the other. Analysts who work with cancer patients may find themselves having death thoughts and concerns about their own health. It is difficult when this occurs to distinguish between induced feelings from the patient and one's own body processes. Working with these feelings is a necessary component of treatment with the severely regressed because it enables the analyst to "know" the impulses and emotional conflicts of the patient.

Szasz (1965) traced a number of somatic disorders to the first two years of life. The analytic community was alerted to the relationship between the level of maturation and the type of enervation to be expected. At the earlier level of development, the sympathetic system is not fully developed; therefore, it would be expected that symptoms would appear related to the parasympathetic systems, symptoms such as diarrhea, asthma, and peptic ulcers. By making this connection between emotional conflict, developmental level, and symptomatology, analysts were given the opportunity to validate assumptions about other connections between physiology and emotion. It was recognized that illnesses connected to the voluntary systems, perceptual and neuromuscular, were related to the inhibition of destructive impulsiveness at varying points along the arousal continuum as a function of the readiness of the organism to use voluntary discharge. According to Alexander (1950), the fantasy of attacking when not physiologically prepared may result in a migraine, whereas if prepared for action, the fantasy may lead to vegetative changes in metabolism and circulation and be accompanied by the development of hypertensive disease.

Alexander (1950) made another connection between preparation for fight when action is impossible and the onset of a muscular inhibition. He found the physiological corollary may be arthritis. Analysts are in a fortunate position to undertake research in this area. As patients present their introspective experiences, they report accompanying perceptions of body functioning. The analyst is in a unique position at the forefront between biology and psychic processes.

As the analyst observes a patient's expressive enervation, he has the opportunity to uncover their connections to emotional life. At the level of pre-object, self/other confusions, we know that physiological pathways of expression are most frequent. In the next chapter, "The Language of Emotion," I discuss the emotional conflicts that a patient often disguises within body symptomatology. Body language has become an important tool in the conduct of an analysis.

Patients do tend to make mental connections between their symptoms and their emotional conflicts. The analyst listens to these indirect communications. For example, I have treated only one blushing patient, but the content of his sessions told me about his perception of object relations and conflicts connected to his sense of self. The ideational content presented by this patient centered on his wish for anal penetration by a phallic mother. He expressed fantasies of being beaten by a powerful woman. These were some of the components of his conscious fantasy life. In the discharge of drives, involuntary enervation such as blushing are expected. We know that hormonal changes occur in erections, ejaculations, and orgasms and that changes in receptivity are accompanied by sexual arousal. It is not unusual to see a patient who is destructively discharging aggressive impulses within his body. When somatizing has been a chronic pattern, we may expect that vegetative disturbances, untreated, will eventuate in organic illnesses and measurable tissue change.

Asthmatics say they feel smothered. They cling to the belief in a loving but demanding or unavailable mother. However, their associations reveal that the smother reaction is a response to the arousal of destructive impulses. To avoid knowing these impulses, they experience terror in interactions with others and object dependency. Rashes are sometimes a portrait of the desire to rid the self of internal poisons. To bring about change with the somatizer, we encourage relief through symbolic representations so that specific emotional contents may be brought closer to discharge through language.

One of my patients presented a repetitive tendency to sigh during sessions. No idea was advanced to explain this phenomenon. She also suffered from a rapid pulse rate and high blood pressure. These are somatic symptoms that appear normally in response to emergency stimulation when the fight/flight responses are stimulated. A body set of fight/flight is their response to bottled-up hostility. In this patient, digestive functions were slowed down, and chronic emotional withdrawal was her preferred defense against her fears. When the process of fight or flight is inhibited, her energy is turned to an historically useful pathway, a somatic one.

The reader may wonder what events in the analytic sessions could bring about relief on the somatic level. We know that neuromuscular or perceptual readiness for fight is less damaging if it can be contained than is vegetative readiness. Thought, created through the process of talking, can relieve some pent-up aggression. Libidinal energy is used to relieve the vegetative symptom while the treatment works through to more productive uses of aggression. The analyst has the responsibility for maintaining a level of stimulation in the sessions that is tolerable to the patient. Otherwise the buildup of intolerable quantities of energy blocks discharge by normal means. In later chapters I discuss the techniques used to match the patient's stimulus level in quantity and kind.

Alexander (1950) connected headaches to the fantasy of attacking behavior. One of my patients who suffers from migraine headaches was able to tell me something about those headaches. She pointed out to me that the time between sessions feels meaningless. She fills it with the tasks that are necessary to keep life going. She said that she tries to keep her mind a void between sessions. To me that meant she does not want to experience me as an object in her head who will arouse longings and not be there. When that happens, she experiences rage and is flooded with revenge fantasies connected with separation, slights, or other painful experiences from previous contacts with people. In this repetitive behavior, the patient does not have many alternatives. She can let an excruciatingly painful person into her head, or she can be alone. The difficulty is keeping the object out. This patient gave me lots of information on how she uses headaches to discharge her hostility and how the headaches serve as a punishment. She explained to me that early in her life, the headaches continued for hours. She would lie in a darkened room seeking some relief from an ice pack on her head. When finally a headache would subside, she would experience a great sense of relief followed by euphoria, even happiness. She replaced thoughts and feelings with pain. The relief was, "Finally, I am rid of it!" This expressed indirectly her wish to be free of object longings.

With the advent of powerful medications for headaches, she was able to eliminate one in an hour or two. The euphoria following the headache also stopped. She misses that feeling. Early in her treatment with me, she had a period in which she was relatively free of headaches, but, later, as she experienced increased feelings of longing, dependence, and disappointment, the migraines returned. Following one of them, a fantasy occurred to her during a session. She was just home from the hospital following her birth. Her mother was unable to walk and had hired a baby-sitter to bring the baby and her bottle to the bed for her feedings. However, in the fantasy, she lay in her crib crying as her mother called out for the baby-sitter who could not be awakened.

As she explained it, she had lots of bad thoughts about her invalid mother that were not justified. She connected her headaches with her objection to acting on unjustified hostility. As treatment progressed, it became clear that she devoted a great deal of energy just before her sessions to keeping bad thoughts out of her mind. She would try not to cry. She would think obsessively to prevent herself from longing for anything. All her energy was devoted to keeping herself in a feelingless state. This attempt to maintain a void was her way of warding off aggression in the service of object/self protection. Unfortunately, this kept her mind and body out of attunement. When this went on for a time, her body expressed what had been blotted out through the painful migraine headache.

As the treatment progressed, she told me more about the headaches. She reported that when a migraine begins, she hears a screaming in her head that she has, over time, connected with words like, "Come, Mommy, hold me." As she tries to empty her head, she screams out, "I'll kill my head to stop crying." From this, it appeared that the headaches were serving a discharge function and, at the same time, conserving energy needed to maintain the void. Instead of letting in the fantasy object, she lets in the symbol for it, the headache. She believes that headaches come when she feels too weak to ward off unwanted thoughts.

From college days to the beginning of her analysis, she reported a connection to her menstrual cycle. In analysis, the headaches preceded the sessions. Thoughts of the session occurred, followed by fantasies of disappointment, and then, as she put it, "Aggression goes bammm." If before a session she has a thought that I should take care of her, the headache starts. She knows it is aggression, but she thinks of herself as passive. She has described herself as a fetus waiting to be dragged into the world. In sessions she runs through her list of what about me bothers her: "If you don't beam at me, I get mad." This seems to sum it up. She wants a physical presence, someone there all the time even though, "It is excruciating to be with you. I guess it is just oneness I want," she adds. A related symptom, present throughout her life, is fainting connected with her most severe migraines. It was during hospitalization for this that she discovered the calming effects of intravenous feedings. Longing to be on IV did not cause the headaches that were created when she longed for objects.

Working with this patient's symptom picture led to further insights into the connection between painful feelings, aggression, and object protection. The severe pain appeared to be a compromise between unbearable thoughts and an empty (of thought and feeling) head.

If this patient could reexperience her longings and allow the fantasy, she, as all somatic patients, would have to do it through experiencing the nuclear conflict in the transference relationship. When a patient is regressed to earliest infancy, the time when nuclear conflicts originate, we find that, barring psychosis, the patient will replace thought with somatic language.

There is a debate in the field on whether schizophrenics experience loneliness. This woman with migraines demonstrates that it is not loneliness that is at issue but aloneness. At the body level, the deepest wish may be to be joined, to exist before the perception of separation occurs in the infant's development. The conflict so dramatically presented by this patient dates to the time an infant discovers he has a separate existence. The times during the treatment when she experiences wanting to get me out of her head alternate with times when she likes being with me. This type of transference is reminiscent of the time of ego development when, emerging from aloneness, the infant becomes aware of painful stimuli and calls them "not me." When a patient enters treatment this regressed, we find that they are leading a bland existence, appearing related, but using most of their creative energy to block feelings.

For the moment, cure of a nuclear conflict begins with control of the tension level in sessions to a level that adaptation to the analytic room does not require somatic outbreaks. This is a crucial first step in the cure of somatic conditions. The strength of the patient's desire to be well is utilized to influence healthier modes of coping with internal pressures. A cautious approach is called for when arousing transference at this level where annihilation, terror, and many other negative states, long unverbalized, have inhibited emotional growth. The goal at this time is to immunize patients from somatic recurrences by increasing their ability to use more mature responses in which affects can be connected with language. Any attempts on the part of patients to discharge destructive impulses against their own bodies is first replaced by language. The patient is helped to describe symbolic representations in simple language. Chronic emotional tension that has led to vegetative disturbances is nipped before it becomes an organic illness. This is accomplished through the connection made between affective experiences and relevant thought processes.

When the migraine patient summed up her core complaint about the analysis, she said that we do not resonate; we are not on the same wavelength. She said also, "I know it is unrealistic. You and I cannot be as one. It is stupid to spend the rest of my life just wanting that with you, wanting to have on my mind whatever is on your mind, but what other solution is there for me?" Repetitively, she convinces herself that I will prevent the resonance and she will be left alone. Over the years, I experienced the feeling that no analytic stance was right for her. Her migraines cheer her up because she prefers to be able to tolerate being alone. The only attraction to a resolution is that she is afraid of nothingness.

We discover anew with our patients that they travel their old pathways in the choice of respiratory, digestive, or circulatory illnesses. On occasion there does not appear to be a specific ideation connected to a particular vegetative disorder. Sometimes we cannot establish links between the patient's physiology and emotions because of the shallowness of our analytic investigations. Long-term analyses have revealed much more to us about these early organic mechanisms of defense than we can hope to reach with short-term treatments. However, the analytic session is the first research tool used to delve into the subjective life in a meaningful way in order to discover connections among emotion, physiological functioning, life strivings, and death. We must concern ourselves with early pathways for the discharge of emotional tension and impulses, with constitutional and environmental factors involved in discharge of emotion as well as their connection with disease and death.

The nuclear conflict just described is one of many seen in treatment. A patient attempting to maintain emotional withdrawal may react to treatment as if it were a straight jacket. Sexual anxiety, itself a defense, may lead to thought blockage and a flow to the body of the sexual conflicts. As analysts working with patients during early regressions, we expect that an adverse therapeutic reaction may lead to somatic responses similar to what is seen in post traumatic reactions. If we discover early in the treatment that a patient resorts to physical paths for tension reduction when over-stimulated by internal or external pressures, we can predict that somatic paths may lead to organic illnesses. When drives have been successfully fused, destructive drives can be subjugated to life constructive goals. Anger, distrust, depression related to hostile or destructive impulsiveness, rage when one is not respected or approved of—all may lead to physiological responses. Another set of emotional concerns may lead to a different set of emotional responses as in conflicts around loving or being loved, intimacy. Other conflicts exist between opposing sets of impulses—for example, the wish to live, the wish to die.

Treatment of a sixty-year-old woman who came complaining of stiff joints presented a clear picture of a proper lady unable to discharge sufficient feeling to release her from the tension states she experienced. Her symptom disappeared and reappeared as a function of the ability to get in touch with feelings. She spoke only of her father in treatment. The very first remission occurred following a question raised by the analyst about rigor mortis. She had disavowed her reaction to her mother's early death and prior emotional unavailability. Instead she developed her own "rigor mortis" in arthritic attacks.

Psychic processes differ from body processes only in that they are experienced subjectively. Conversely, the absence of subjective feelings leaves only the somatic pathway open for the discharge of impulses. Although psychic ideas cannot be directly transposed into physiological responses any more than physiology can be transposed into psychic phenomena, we are learning that transformations are possible in ways not yet entirely clear.

More recently, we have seen that symptoms such as headaches serve to drain off some of the instinctual tensions. Hysterical conversions can be connected directly to unconscious processes. They are a displaced expression of impulses, with the conversion serving as a direct symbolic expression of a specific emotional content. Vegetative responses do not so clearly reveal the specific wish hidden behind the somatic symptom. We do know that vegetative disease can be caused by chronic unrelieved emotional tension; we know that conflicts connected with infancy are related to survival. While conversions relieve in a symbolic, displaced way, physical disorders demonstrate that the body and mind may respond interchangeably to stimulation from either sphere. This interchangeability can be studied when we work with psychotic patients. We have learned that preverbal conflicts can be discharged along somatic pathways if the ability to fantasize is underdeveloped as in schizophrenia. Schizophrenia relies on denial of external stimulation and avoidance mechanisms to blot out the part that comes from inside. Somatization occurs when these mechanisms fail.

If we think of the patient's defense structure in energy terms, we look at each defense as a control on the quantity of stimulation and the tension level that is tolerable. Since symptoms tend to drain off some energy, the individual with no other outlet can resort to somatic channels for expression.

CHAPTER THREE

~

The Language of Emotion

How the Mind Unfolds

When a psychoanalyst speaks of regressed, infantile, or narcissistic patients, it is difficult to describe how, in the absence of adequate language, the patient conveys his emotional conflicts. Since the preverbal patient cannot tell us what he experiences, analysts find it necessary to develop other tools to uncover the root of the patient's disturbances. Words too often confuse as well as communicate. The language of the severely disturbed has often been described as word salad. At best, it is a symbolic expression of meaning that cannot be conveyed directly.

When a patient experiences the world as dangerous or persecutory, we can expect that he does not want to be overstimulated by the analyst. I remember Bobby who was brought into my clinic at five years old, diagnosed as autistic. I opened the toy closet and sat down. There was a small chair close to mine. His choice was clear. He could sit in the small chair, or he could play with toys that interested him. He selected a rubber dagger and a toy soldier and proceeded to repetitively stab the toy soldier with the knife. He dropped the soldier to the floor and said, "Dead." Within moments he swept the soldier up, cradled him in his arms, and cooed to him. He repeated this procedure, over and over. Bobby used other repetitive actions. He would turn the light switch off, pause, look around, and then turn it on again. At times he appeared agitated. He would then sit down, stare ahead, and rock against the wall, saying, "I'm Bobby, I'm Bobby." After he had been coming for a while, the words

47

sounded different. Instead of blandly saying, "I'm Bobby" as though into a void, he varied the intonations. Sometimes he seemed tentative, and I thought he was speaking to me. Once when I replied, saying, "Are you Bobby?" he said, "Bobby, Bobby," and laughed. Later, I introduced sound when he stabbed the soldier: "Ooh, ooh." He responded by holding the soldier for a moment longer before he again stabbed it and threw it to the floor. It was through touch and sound that nuances of meaning developed between us. At each slight change in Bobby's behavior, he showed pleasure. He enjoyed playing with sounds, and when I echoed a sound, he began to notice me. It was a learning process in sharing for both of us. This is how Bobby occupied himself, session after session, until one day, the director said he needed the room that Bobby and I used. We were assigned another room, and when Bobby arrived, he was escorted there. He looked around terrified then ran to a darkened corner, sat on the floor facing the door, banged his head and back against the wall, and screamed, over and over, "I'm Bobby, I'm Bobby." The terror was exactly as it had been at the start of treatment. What explained the regression? Could a change of room be the explanation? Was a new environment too stimulating? Was any change in routine something that could not be immediately mastered? Had I betrayed him? Unfortunately, his parents ended the sessions, and I did not have the opportunity to go further with Bobby. What was possible between us and pleasantly stimulating changed in this experience to something overstimulating. Bobby and I had not worked together long enough to develop more words for our emotional exchanges. I believe that aural and tactile sensations were felt as contacts and that, in time, Bobby would have put words to acts as he learned to be emotionally connected. However, from Bobby I did learn that to discriminate what one feels is the base on which each of us builds our memories, our language, and our relationships. The effect of a change of room for Bobby was global. He could have experienced a wide range of reactions, but terror appeared to dominate. If any change means betrayal and terror, how can analysts create an environment that allows for growth?

The Developing Mind

Analysts were confounded about the treatment of severely regressed patients. Thoughts differed on what constitutes personality. Before the development of language, tension states are expressed through the body. Freud (1920) sought an answer to why people destroy or harm themselves and take pleasure in their own destruction. Why do we see patients who cut their skin to bleed or rub their skin raw with emory boards? Freud's (1919, 1920) investigation of masochism and sadism led him to the theory of life and death drives. He found that in pathology the two separate sets of drives work against each other and in mental health work cooperatively. He discovered this relation through his work on masochism. The treatment of masochism required finding out why a patient could not turn aggression outward but instead turned it against the self. Later analysts, studying depression, noted that patients accused themselves, saying to the analyst, "You are a fine analyst. There is something wrong with me that you cannot help me. It is all my fault." Some people never progress so far as depression. Prior to the development of an "I" able to create an image of a worthless self, patients express conflict through their bodies and in body symptoms.

Another early attempt to control destructive impulses, used in paranoia, is to project parts of the self-image onto others, seeing these parts as external to "me." It is "he" who likes to hurt people, not "me." Freud (1926) revised his earlier theory of anxiety as the expression of thwarted libido to anxiety as a signal of danger. Originally anxiety was a result of repression, not a signal to initiate a defense against a danger. Was it a danger based on the memory of a past traumatic moment, or was it a danger in the present moment resulting from internal flooding of excitation too overpowering to achieve sufficient discharge? When pressed by internal need, the body, which experiences tension, struggles to unload the oppressive quantity of stimulation and to achieve a pleasurable calm. Historically, danger and anxiety were thought of as results of external causes, not internal drive states. That an infant could be overwhelmed by his own destructive drives; that prior to having an image of a mother whom he wanted to please, could be conflicted about his own drives, was hard to accept and did not make sense until Freud (1920) realized the opposition of life and death forces. In pathology these forces are not fused so they continue to war with each other. This finding stirred excitement in the psychoanalytic community. Analysts debated the curative power of reconstructing the past when drive arousal, anxiety, and defense were alive and observable in the present. A rash of publications followed for and against dropping theories of reconstruction as the curative factor in treatment. The arguments over a theory of aggression and Freud's (1926) revised theory of signal anxiety ripped the field asunder, leading to distinct "schools of thought" within psychoanalysis. Should we give up caring about the content of the patient's life, forget about reconstructing the past, and concentrate only on analyzing the transference? Some analysts stated that if conflicts are not brought "live" into the room in the patient's thoughts and feelings toward the analyst, analysis cannot lead to change. When the patient says what he believes he is conflicted about, the analyst understands that much is missing from the patient's conscious presentation, the fuller truth hidden behind the patient's defenses.

A patient may report having trouble with people because they don't understand him or are prejudiced against him. He does not usually say to the analyst, "You see how I provoke people to react to me the way they do." He demonstrates his provocativeness in his interactions with the analyst.

The philosophical papers written by Freud in the last decade of his life clarified the meaning of life/death. Analysts have since struggled, much as Freud (1926) did, in thinking through their implications. Both analyst and patient prefer to think of human difficulties as problems with mothers, girl and boyfriends, or children. If a patient is fairly mature, he has probably settled into a characterological way of resolving conflict. His defensive armoring maintains his mental processes. He may have repressed conflicts, unaware of emotions that bother him; developed reaction formations, stressing the acceptable side of his ambivalence; or sublimated, engaging in activities that provide substitute gratification of drives. However, he comes to treatment because drive satisfaction is not complete enough, life is not as satisfying as it should be, or the defenses are crumbling.

In his later life, Freud (1930) suggested Eros and Thanatos in conflict, rather than libido theory, as the best explanation of the behavior of adults struggling with pathological fixations from the time of structuring a mind. Many wondered why Freud (1920) posited a second group of primary instincts. Fenichel (1953), his student, questioned whether it wasn't sufficient to say people are destructive when frustrated. Why was it necessary to go beyond libido theory with its two components, sex and self-preservation? Analysts provided clinical evidence to support the explanatory power of libido theory. When a four-year-old cannot have an ice cream cone, he flies into a tantrum and fantasizes about destruction. Libido theory explains his reaction: frustration of pleasure. In the course of further mental development, the desire to be loved, to be praised, not to be abandoned holds his impulses and fantasies in check. Being good, after all, carries its own rewards. For many years, analysts were satisfied with the single drive explanation of human behavior. Life was seen as a struggle between libidinal/sexual pleasures and society's prohibitions. Frustration was the result. However, libido theory troubled analysts. How to explain anxiety and the retreat from one's own impulses during the first years of life and in regressed states when society's values have not yet been internalized and functioning occurs in a nonobject framework.

Part of the difficulty in thinking of drives is that we never see them. They are, in fact, as Freud (1933b) himself said, our "mythology." We think of drives as the source in our body from which instinctual needs emerge. What can be observed of drives is the search for relief from the arousal. In truth, we cannot say that we observe the drives; we observe an intolerable tension that demands discharge.

As soon as one begins to think of a patient in terms of drives, interest turns to the nature of discharge patterns and the objects selected to express desire. Many drives can be discharged within the body, but hunger and thirst require an outside something for satisfaction. In infancy, satisfaction is attempted through hallucinatory wish fulfillment and fantasy. But these usually prove disappointing. As Freud (1910b) pointed out, "Such measures, however, have as much influence on the symptoms of nervous illness as a distribution of menu-cards in a time of famine has upon hunger" (255).

A new world opened when analysts began to think in terms of dual drives. The theory provided explanatory power as to why one may need to form negative relations with others. A study of the gradual evolving mind reveals the process by which we select from our experiences the direction to pursue in order to satisfy our drives. The eventual character observed in treatment is the product of the interaction between drives as well as between drive and defense, and it will be revealed in the transference. Character will be formed and if frozen will dictate a repetitive pattern through which partial satisfaction is sought in the world. The role of the environment in this process is to provide a range of possibilities from which to choose. Drive is a result of biology; character is a result of that biology interacting with the possibilities life offers.

When an analyst, in his office, observes a character, it turns out to be more difficult to speak diagnostically of an oral, anal, or phallic fixation. Solutions from these levels of development remain a part of character and will appear even in maturity. They find means of expression by combining with each other and, at times, by replacing each other. In other words, part of development is the displacement and fusion of drive states.

Once Freud (1920) had offered a theory of dual drives, it was necessary to explain why behavior is rarely purely destructive or purely constructive but a combination of the two sets. Think of constructing a building. Part of the pleasure is in seeing the rooms come together, seeing the doors hung so they can swing freely, seeing the paint applied, but part of the pleasure in this "construction" comes from tearing down the old structures as in sledgehammering a wall marked for demolition. For as long as we can remember, wars have served a similar function for men. Hopefully we will find activities that combine both sets of drives that do not require the annihilation of others. Thinking in terms of fusion and defusion of drives aided clinicians because it explained what they observed in their patients. Personality is built on compromise through the fusion of drives and, in later development, when the conflict is between drive and defense rather than between drives, through compromise with defensive positions.

In pathology one sees a predominance of self-destructiveness, but this is combined with a fear of one's own destructiveness toward others. The dominance of destructiveness in the personality varies from individual to individual. Its expression is determined partly from genetic history, partly from temperament, partly from intrauterine experience, and partly from life after birth. Of these, temperament is the most difficult to influence, since it represents the quantitative balance between life and death drives, the nuclear conflict seen in early phases of personality development. The interaction of the drives and temperament controls the unfolding of each particular mind.

We know infants are dominated by drives pressing for discharge and that when the pressure is great or the drive is experienced as dangerous, the anxiety or tension level may lead to a withdrawal from the stimulation. A defense may block discharge or lead to symptoms. At an early stage in life, defenses used to counter an impulse may be somatic or, as in psychosis, a confusion of mind, an inability to think clearly.

To understand anxiety and defensiveness in narcissistic persons, analysts found that the concept of instincts led them to understand prelanguage behavior as a reaction to overstimulation in the body or to more excitement than the body can process. In thinking about early functioning, analysts concurring with Freud's life–death balance interpreted the death instinct as a need to escape from overstimulation.

Those who accepted instinct theory observed excitation in the body as a pressure for discharge of quantities of energy. Excitation is sometimes discharged into the body and sometimes through the body. Satisfaction shows in body change when tension states have been reduced successfully.

Because analysts were beginning to recognize that the infantile psyche is coping with dangerous overload, new ideas emerged to explain how the mind unfolds. In Freud's (1926) modified theory of anxiety as a danger signal, the connection was made to the concept of an overload of excitation. Freud's dual drive theory had already introduced many complications into how analysts explained their patients. Now analysts had to deal with innate aggression sometimes turned against the self, sometimes turned toward others and the external world. Recognizing that there are unconscious urges to destroy led analysts to consider dangers to themselves in the transference and led many to place their chairs closer to the door for a faster escape should impulsive urges of the patient get out of control. Analysts had to recognize that what transpires between them and patients is not usually a love affair but an attempt to control these dangerous impulses. The notion that drives may conflict with each other expanded analytic theory. It presented a much more complex picture of the patients' experiences than the simple conflict between sexual wishes and life preservation.

Fusion theory portrayed human behavior as a struggle for dominance between forces seeking stimulation and those seeking diminishment of stimulation. No longer was it sufficient to see the patient as trying to cope with pressure to behave in socially appropriate ways. In the new theory, drives to increase tension struggle against drives for discharge. Health can be achieved through actions that integrate both tendencies, to build up and to tear down. The compromise formation requires some satisfaction for both tendencies.

Freud's (1905b) early examples were easy to understand. If an infant felt an impulse to strike out, hit or bite and he experienced the impulse as a powerful urge, normally he would discharge the urge or repress it. Much to our surprise, we discovered not only are most early instincts experienced as a pressure to discharge in order to relieve the body of excitation, but also the very act of discharge is experienced as dangerous. This appears to be true early in life before fear of external figures can account for the perception of drive discharge as dangerous. It took from the 1930s to very recently to accept the idea that the natural pull to discharge of excitation opposes the libidinal pull to life and excitement.

What could this mean for analytic work? For reasons we cannot comprehend, a struggle exists between impulses to live and impulses to reduce tension. A theory advanced by Freud (1926) was that in the creation of human life, drive states were activated to continue the alive state. The discomfort of living—that is, the tension states that press for lowering tension—are confronted by this opposing desire to tolerate excitation with its unpleasure and to live. The discovery of this conflict state between life and death made it possible for analysts to learn a great deal about the relationship between internal dangers from impulses arising in the body, and the danger perceived as coming from external sources. Analysts recognized that the fear of internal dangers from our own impulses had to be displaced because so long as the danger was seen as internal, there was no way to avoid it. What we learned was that high states of excitation in the body of the preverbal child were experienced as unpleasurable simply because they were perceived as more stimulating than the immature psyche could process and were therefore incapable of discharge.

When impulses are aroused, the infant has a fantasy of satisfaction that is accompanied by sensations of danger. What we call the individual's character are the patterns developed in rejecting impulses. By seeing the danger as external to the body, as though coming from the environment, one had the option of taking flight and avoiding the external temptation perceived as causing danger. Depending on the age and development of the infant, the danger takes a specific form—for example, fear of the traumatic moment of birth with its memory traces of overstimulation, fear of loss or abandonment in the oral stage of helplessness and dependency, or fear of castration in the oedipal struggle for connectedness. Each fear is connected with a maturational stage of development in which there is increasing awareness of helplessness and dependency on the outside world. Knowing that drives for connectedness exist alongside drives to disconnect helped analysts to understand the relation among fear of punishment, fear of objects, fear of satisfaction, and the signal of impending danger connected to one's own impulses. Understanding this dynamic helped modern analysts to work with patients' fears.

Instinctual urges when denied discharge may persist and continue to press for discharge or may be destroyed, thus freeing the energy to travel other pathways. In one pathological solution, a regression takes place allowing the impulse to revert to earlier used means of discharge. This regression results when the pleasure principle is replaced by a repetition of the struggle between discharge and prohibition when the power of the internal stimulation threatens the psychic system. Such traumatic moments were long believed by analysts to be part of psychic life once development progressed to the ability to store memories of painful experiences.

The threat of repetition of pain is seen in later developmental stages as a danger to be avoided because of this remembered experience of pain. What was new in Freud's (1926) later work on anxiety was the recognition of anxiety dating from birth when language, memory, and object awareness do not exist.

Talking Symbolically through Fantasy and Dream

When a severely regressed patient enters treatment with what we call a narcissistic transference, we expect a different kind of transference than what is seen in the treatment of neurotic cases. It is what the patient transfers to the analyst that is used to reach the unconscious. The patient will speak to the analyst out of hidden fantasies, essentially unconscious, in which he shapes his current experience to mirror those parts of himself that are in conflict. He does not relate to the analyst as the bad mother or father of history who abused him but through symbolic creations which acquaint the analyst with the nature of the patient's internal struggle with his own impulses. When we work within the narcissistic transference, it is not our goal to reconstruct the patient's past. What concerns the analyst is why the parts of the self that are denied and projected have to be excluded from the patient's self-understanding.

We want to know the motive! In how the patient behaves with the analyst, we will learn which of his impulses he cannot face. The particular personality organization the analyst will work with is revealed in the transference. An underlying motive was revealed to me by a patient who, when angry in the transference, shouted, "I want to be part of a loyal family!"

How the patient sees the other person in the room reflects some part of the patient's self. To take away his defensive posture through interpretation can lead to still deeper regression, possibly to somatic symptomatology. Much research has been conducted that reveals how under the pathological condition of regression somatic symptoms may appear. Looking back on the history of psychoanalysis, we wonder why, for so many years, analysts felt the need to interpret these symptoms to the patient.

It was not until the 1950s at the Jewish Board of Guardians that Spotnitz (1976) developed the approach to patients that came to be known as joining or emotional communication, in which the patients' protective devices are preserved as long as needed. In the 1970s and 1980s when institutes sent analytic candidates to study in mental hospitals, it was discovered that staff was still being trained to confront psychotic patients with reality, showing them the purposes of their maladaptive behavior and asking them to give it up. Learning to be with patients in ways that help them to gain control over destructive impulsiveness has required that the analyst be aware of his own impulses. Much of analytic training has been devoted to developing this skill.

A supervisee told me she was not sure what was meant when we spoke of emotional communication with a severely regressed patient. She wondered how one could be sure just what was being communicated. As an example, she reported a session about a patient who always imagined being behind bars and that he and his wife had to have sex between the bars. One day, he fantasized that he was out from behind the bars and made love to his wife. His wife was very disturbed by this, so he retreated behind the bars. That, the supervisee reported, was his fantasy. She added that in general he is detached and blocked. In the fantasy he makes it clear that he is protecting his wife. He gives the message that he stays behind bars in order to protect her and the marriage. The therapist felt she must interpret this fantasy, so in the next group session she asked the patient, "What does one do when he believes that his emotions may be too strong for the other person?" In saying this to his whole therapy group, she demonstrated one way that an analyst may respond to an emotional (symbolic) communication. In this case the patient feels that his sexual needs are a burden to his wife. In development, this is one way the child responds to his own impulses. They may be burdensome to someone else. The therapist used her understanding of the patient from her long contact with him and the emotion conveyed in the fantasy to show him that she was aware of his internal distress at disturbing his wife. The purpose of her communication (a question) was to help him and the others to begin a dialogue in which he could face his distress and put words to it. Over the course of the treatment, she had seen the same distress in his transference to her but had not brought his feelings to his attention in their relationship. By bringing it to the group's attention, she conveyed an understanding of the pain caused by his own impulses. Correctly, she refrained from asking him whether he felt imprisoned in the analytic relationship. This she recognized would attack the primitive defenses, defenses that made it possible for him to be in the room with her and to communicate his dilemma symbolically.

In treatment, analysts are aware that patients fear their impulses when they are regressed, particularly when they are regressed to the first year of life when language skills are undeveloped. When impulses press for expression at this stage of development, they call up the most primitive of defenses (e.g., somatization, denial, projection, and introjection). The analyst learns through what the patient brings to sessions which parts of the patient's experience are avoided or denied and which parts are projected in the transference to the analyst. What a patient projects onto the analyst may be an archaic good imago, a bad imago, some combination of them, or parts of the self. The analyst can be omnipotent, benevolent, or caring in the patient's view but can also be hostile, demanding, devouring, or neglectful. These parts of the self we think of as the first impressions experienced by the infant in his dealings with the environment. They exist as parts of the self confused with images of objects and are projected as the dangerous external terrain. What the patient cannot experience as 'me' or as a part of his or her internal experience is first called 'you' in the treatment, and in negotiations with the external world, she or he views these internal experiences as coming from the external object.

Analytically, the patient's perceptions are accepted, his views of the analyst not contradicted. In the dialogue that ensues, the analyst, instead of explaining what the analyst views as projections, reflects the patient's perceptions in questions to the patient. One of the earliest bad imagoes to be projected is the 'unavailable object'. The baby who has repetitive experiences of no response to her pain will fear the loss of the omnipotent provider. The danger she experiences is that she is helpless.

The analyst studies the patient's way of handling this helplessness. Does he perceive the analyst as omnipotent? Through oneness with the analyst does he recapture the feeling that he is both the feeder and the fed, sufficient onto himself? If the patient projects omnipotence to the analyst and feels loved by the analyst, does he regain a sense of his own power? In some cases the patient appears to be fascinated by the analyst hanging on her every word; in others he experiences the analyst as dangerous. He may cringe when he first comes into the analyst's presence at the beginning of each session. These behaviors reflect the end of the early oral stage of development when the individual discovers he needs someone or something other than himself in order to survive. In the earlier stage of helplessness, there is not the experience of an object to meet needs; there is no 'me' or 'not me'. The early infantile perceptions delay the concept of a separate self through oral incorporation. This is replaced soon by a biting phase in which the infant experiences ambivalence both toward his impulse and toward the rejecting presence that is beginning to come into focus. Later, in his insecurity and his recognition that he does not alone have the skill to get his needs met, he will begin to concentrate on himself and fear his own inadequacy.

By the next maturational level, a conflict develops as the object is finally seen, and seen as good or bad. During this, the anal sadistic phase, the small child is torn between possessing and destroying the object. In a later phase of childhood beginning in latency, the child perceives the strictures against his impulses as coming from the outside world. He suffers from moral anxiety and a fear of punishment. As the reality principle gains a foothold in his thinking, these anxieties diminish but are never gone entirely. Ultimately the particular emotional illness seen in the adult is a result of the fixation point in the individual's character.

We understand a patient's symbolic communications in terms of which maturational phase is represented as causing pain. You might ask, What is the danger that frightens people suffering from neurotic anxiety? The answer simply stated is unconsummated excitation that leads to anxiety. As a patient struggles with a particular impulse, he conjures up images of the dangers, and they tell him the activity that must be stopped. Different individuals respond differently to this message. One may develop a symptom; another will go so far as to express a preference for an opposite impulse. The anxiety that signals displeasure could simply lead to a withdrawal from the objectionable excitation. A defense may be erected against consciously experiencing what is wanted. The more mature individual will resort to fantasy and thinking when unpleasant feelings surface. In these ways, he can anticipate satisfactions.

The development of a symptom is seen clearly in the case of phobias. In a phobia the individual replaces his fear of his impulses with a real and external danger. The symptom becomes a necessary alternative when internally there is no way to escape the pressure for discharge from the impulse. In his report on Little Hans, Freud (1909a) connected the fear of going in the streets because of the dangerous horses to the impulses Hans had repressed regarding his father. Analysts recognize that symptom and anxiety are interchangeable; therefore, to deprive a patient of a symptom (e.g., a compulsion to wash her hands or check the gas jets) is to invite regression to escape the anxiety that is unbound when the symptom is removed.

I remember having to deal with a full-blown schizophrenic reaction in a patient who used alcohol as a way of coping. He would report to a routine job every day and return home at five to begin drinking beer. Twelve to fifteen bottles later he would fall into a stupor and sleep it off overnight. A colleague encouraged the patient to go to a rehabilitation center for alcoholics. Over the course of the year, feeling attached to the colleague, he gave up drinking. When he was discharged from the program, he felt adrift and depressed. First, he gave up working, later he feared leaving the house. When a friendly young woman moved in with him, she brought him for a consultation. By this time, he was suspicious, fear alternating with detachment and occasional delusions. He had no interest in taking care of his body, in working, or in relating. Who knows how long he could have survived as an alcoholic, but now he was certainly in a worse place. Had he worked analytically prior to the stopping of his drinking, we might have seen a different picture.

When a patient comes into treatment, it is possible for a transference to be instantly aroused and for the patient to experience his longings directly in the analysis. This was true of a student in one of my classes. The first week, she sat twitching nervously, in pain. Abruptly she was on her feet running from the room. She returned apologizing, saying, "I had to vomit." When this occurred a second time, I began to question, "What does she have to spit out? What cues were stimulating this level of rejection?"

I treated a woman who said that the kind of relief she needed could only be achieved if her analyst would meet her needs, but she feels she should not be burdening her analyst. She should not want what she wants. Beyond that, she fears being thought of as a spoiled rotten bitch. This patient is no exception. When a patient is in transference, he longs for things. What is longed for will be whatever is missing. It may be what was once his and was lost, or it may be for something never possessed. The transference situation is reminiscent of the mother–infant situation. At what stage in that relationship does a mother give the infant what he wants? Before an infant has learned to walk or talk, he deals with needs that are difficult to express. The needs result in tension that is overstimulating. The infant doesn't know how to reduce the tension and to experience satisfaction. To survive infants begin the process of identifying a caretaker 'out there' who can control the situation for them. It is a slow learning process in infancy until the environment can be perceived as able to deliver what is needed.

One of the results of this dependency is to begin to long for the presence of that external force for comfort. This is an early act of awareness of the 'other'. The existence of hunger pangs changes the world from "me alone" to "me and you." For infants, hunger and cold coordinate with smell and touch to create a vision of the breast or a touch and the pain-free state. We say of infants that they have begun the process of building a mind. What this infant brings as an adult to treatment is fixed ways of perceiving solutions to his internal dilemmas.

In treatment we observe how an individual deals with needs that arouse helplessness or inadequacy. We study how emotional lives are organized around conflicting drive states. If an analyst makes the decision to work with severely regressed patients, he should plan to do more than make the unconscious conscious. In fact, the unconscious may be better known by psychotic than neurotic patients. What will be involved is a restructuring of the mind. An overwhelming task? Yes, if we cannot uncover the mystery of the pathology. We observe how the patient copes with difficulty, how he perceives self and other and relationships, how he judges external events and organizes experience because all his current methods will be changed in the course of a lengthy analysis.

Modern analytic technique stresses that the analyst's presence in the treatment room be nonthreatening. The patient is encouraged to express his own understanding of his current functioning. In this approach, it is taken as a given that the patient's perception of the outside world will be limited by his internal states. His options will be limited by his hidden conflicts. It is the analyst's goal to help the patient to broaden his understanding of himself and the world as far as he wishes to go toward the freedom to know what he wants and how to achieve it.

When analysts first interned in American mental hospitals, they were confronted with the psychiatric goal of introducing the psychotic patient to 'the reality principle'. It was clear this drove the patients deeper into psychotic thinking. This led the hospitals to increase or change the drug dosages.

Patients cling tenaciously to a view of the external world that contains the rejected parts of their inner world. What the patient says about us or his surroundings is based not in reality but in an individual and unique construction of the world. You might say we are studying each individual's private theater. Everything we hear when the patient speaks has to do with the patient's unsatisfied needs and his solutions to his personal dilemma.

Everything we observe when with an infant or a patient tells us about his unsatisfied needs and how bombarded he feels. He will report feeling pressured, or anxious, or confused. His mental state is one of overstimulation. Does an analyst want to work with seriously regressed patients? In the heyday of psychoanalysis analysts said no. They preferred to work with highly organized patients struggling with some minor feelings of dissatisfaction. Leo Stone (1954) once mentioned a man who consulted an analyst because of a reaction he had to eating lobster, the development of rare headaches. Stone suggested that if such a man has a successful work and home life, appears healthy and relatively happy, he should give up eating lobster rather than undertake a psychoanalysis. To decide whether a patient needs analysis, it is worthwhile to consider the patient's motivation to know himself better. That combined with the analyst's willingness to work with him, should warrant a "go." If the patient states a goal with which the analyst feels she can work, the two have established a basis for agreement to start treatment.

Spotnitz, who developed modern analysis, began writing and lecturing on what makes work with regressed patients particularly interesting. When a person is capable of some self-appraisal, as opposed to a constant rationalization of his actions, analytic movement becomes possible. Analysts have come to believe that a patient's strong desire to undertake an analysis should be a primary consideration in beginning one.

Patients should give thought to the qualities of the person consulted for analysis. How can the patient judge whether this analyst is capable of carrying out a successful analysis? Analysts learn again and again that despite technical training, what counts is the ability to care about the persons in treatment. However, to care must be considered a limitation when used improperly in the interchanges with the patient. To be cured the patient requires a genuine interest that does not result in overstimulation, as for example, in reassuring a patient that everything will work out, that it is just a feeling and will pass, or that the patient is fine. What a patient needs when dealing with a bad feeling is the belief that his analyst knows how difficult his feelings are for him.

Spotnitz (1969, 1985) discovered that all forms of reassurance can lead to self-hatred in the patient. He believed that a different kind of neutrality is required. Rather than offering excessive praise or other overly supportive interventions, he suggests emotional communications that reflect the patient's actual impressions of his situation. He recognized that showing the patient love when the patient hates can be too out of touch with his struggles with destructive fantasies.

Using intuition to make the correct communications to the patient should result in the patient feeling understood or, for the more deeply regressed, feeling at 'one' with the analyst. The intuitions to which Spotnitz (1969, 1985) refers are seen as a result of the analyst's caring about the emotional health of his patient. It is only the loving feelings experienced toward the patient that make it possible to put up with the long periods of negative reactions as the patient uses his primitive defenses to cope.

Love allows the analyst to use negative feelings in his interchanges with patients. Love combined with assertiveness should shape the interventions. As in chess, the goal is to take the queen and stalemate the king, but as you play you cannot reveal your strategies. The game in analysis is to defeat the illness that the patient is determined to keep. Because the transference and countertransference feelings in narcissism are predominately negative for large portions of the treatment, the positive must be discovered when the analyst is away from the sessions and can contemplate what is going on.

One of the experiences with such patients is an appreciation of their tenacity and their courage when in the throes of a pathological condition. We note with appreciation the patient's stick-to-it-ness. Some of his characteristics give us the strength to go the next round. Occasionally, the patient will give up a defensive position to move to some clarity, and, again, the analyst appreciates the patient's courage. It is these feelings that counterbalance the motives inspired by the patient. The patient may not wish to be portrayed as someone an analyst can barely put up with. Don't forget, we are talking about periods in the treatment when a patient is regressed to early fixation points dominated by self-rejection and the desire to destroy all around him. The defenses keep the patient from acting on the extremes of his most destructive impulses, but the feelings stimulated in the analyst can reflect the most hateful feelings that the patient is defending against.

Interpretations can be offered as emotional communications in order to stay in tune with a regressed patient. Treatment is not supportive in its usual sense but works on a "twin image" concept. The patient's hidden desires will be found acceptable by him over time as he observes the analyst's ability to accept a range of feelings. As in good mothering, the analyst is in no rush to dissolve the patient's resistances to saying everything and knowing all. He recognizes that resolution comes through acceptance of what the patient is experiencing at each stage of his unfolding. Modern analysis for the most part has eliminated the major interventions of ego analysis, the tendency to give the patient information about his defensive operations. Although one sees the necessity to familiarize oneself with each patient's defensive style, no value is seen in providing intellectual insights into these patterns. This fits with the modern tendency to deemphasize the role of diagnosis in the timing of interventions. We are concerned about whether a patient, when given an address, can find his way to the analyst's office. Sound obvious? Getting there has many emotional ramifications that can be explored or handled in a nonstimulating manner. Does the patient come on time? What help does he need with that? If a patient is asked how he comes to be here in the analyst's office, he may say he came by subway, missing the intent of the question. The analyst may ask a different question: "Did he have a reason for wanting to see me?" In asking these questions the analyst is, in a sense, making a diagnosis, but it is not a psychiatric category. One wants to judge how it will be possible for the patient to come to sessions and in a timely fashion. The analyst is interested in how the patient pays or doesn't pay for sessions and whether he can talk with some consistency. If he says his mind is blank, what can resolve this resistance, and how patiently should it be handled? Again, diagnosis is ongoing. We see that the patient has certain characteristics. They appear more or less difficult to work with. Giving a name to the disease entity does not change the necessity to understand characteristic by characteristic.

Some patients want a diagnosis. They talk anxiously for a session or two then ask, "What is my diagnosis?" The analyst may ask, "Are you phobic, are you schizophrenic, are you in a psychotic depression?" to which the patient may respond, "I hope not!" or "That's very perceptive of you." In response to the psychotic depression question, the patient may say, "Well, I don't feel depressed." In initial sessions, the analyst makes note of inordinate sensitivity, body rigidity, and negative therapeutic reactions. He is alert for deep anxiety or insecurity, disturbances in reality testing, and the use of projection in describing the events of his life. These traits help the analyst think about how the treatment should begin in a manner that will avoid direct onslaught of a patient's defensive maneuvers. As analysts, we have discovered using the feelings induced by patients helps us in understanding what our responses will mean to the patient. If I feel detached, sleepy, or empty inside, I believe I am feeling the patient's feelings when in a narcissistic void. If I feel the urge to lay down rules for the patient or to obsess about proper behavior, I may be reacting to the obsessional or rigid nature of the patient's character. Using my feelings when reexperienced over time helps me to discover feelings that the patient hides from or behind.

In narcissism there are a number of ways to express destructive impulses. A patient may attack himself, he may obliterate his mind and lose his ability to think, or he may attack his personality, describing himself as worthless. He can find numerous ways of turning aggression against the self. Most vividly, patients may cut themselves or in other ways do damage to their bodies. These acts turn most people away from them.

We see many patients who have moved beyond the early oral phase but are caught in maladaptive ways of forming relationships. Some are only able to be with others when they are drunk; some are with people but caught up in perversions and various forms of sexual acting out. Eventually in the analysis an analyst can say, regarding the most destructive forms of behavior reported repetitively, what a parent says to a child, "I would prefer it if you could refrain from doing that." To sit silently while a patient describes destructive acts can be misunderstood as passive acceptance. It also ignores the reason in the transference for repetitions bringing destructiveness to the attention of the analyst.

Some define treatability, when the behavior is extreme, by the patient's ability to consider certain tendencies as an illness. It is certainly easier to work with a patient who wants to work on a particular piece of pathology, but to achieve this may not always be possible.

I had a successful Hollywood producer whose pictures dealt with themes of incest and murder come to treatment. He was able to tolerate and be in touch with his most primitive thoughts and feelings. He could engage in perverse acts without guilt. He sought help for headaches that caused blackouts. His first sentence to me in the first session was, "If you ever do anything to interfere with my sexual life, I will leave. I am coming here for my head." He wanted to be a patient only if I thought it was possible to treat his headaches. He did not want to touch any other issues.

I do not think of eliminating a patient from consideration because he places restrictions on what he is willing to work on. Much work can be done on why a patient has headaches. If, on the other hand, he wants sessions to get a desperate wife off his back or to comply with a court order and I can find no other goal operating, the indications for a successful treatment are not good. Some psychopathic individuals with no motivation for internal change come and experience the analyst as the 'skin mother' or a reflection of the self. That is often sufficient to overcome the lack of motivation.

All the patients who seek us out are stuck at one or another stage of development, and there are remnants of all the other levels still operable in their characters. If they are stuck at fantasies of good and bad archaic imagoes and unable to function in real relationships, they can be treated in this preobject state using the narcissistic transference and countertransference.

These treatments are not easy. A man I have seen over twelve years has just begun telling me I am one of two people with whom he feels safe. He is certain that no matter how much I know about how bad he is, I will not do anything to harm him. He has begun talking about how destructive he believes he is. He provides me with plenty of examples to illustrate how he behaves with others.

It is clear he fears the intensity of his feelings. This is a man beginning to come out of his isolation. He lives alone, works alone, goes about his work satisfactorily, but cannot be with other people. Feeling connected is a new feeling for him. Feeling he won't be abandoned, he believes he can take more chances in revealing himself. However, he is not sure what he might be capable of doing. This was the secret behind his wall of detachment and isolation. Much as the phobic avoids certain situations, he avoids contacts that might lead to acting on impulses. If required to be in a situation with other people, his goal is to get in and out as quickly as possible. Progress in analysis leads to radical new discoveries about human motivation.

Many analysts solve parental and marital problems or give advice, rather than take the hard road to helping patients function on their own by getting at the motives behind their failures. When a patient asks an analyst to "do it for me," the analyst interested in cure will determine the motive behind this request. However, some needs that appear in the transference are met. The analyst provides the patient with a listener. He establishes conditions that will be favorable to the development of transference, and he conveys that he is dedicated to resolving resistance to successful functioning by starting the treatment, helping the patient to stay and to develop the transference, working through blocks to talking through the use of analytic exploration and emotional communication based on induced countertransference feelings that guide him to an understanding of the patient's experiences.

In connection with what the analyst does, one trainee asked what one does about patients who don't live up to the contract to come regularly, to arrive on time, to pay, and to lie on the couch. He had a patient who consistently came late. I told him that sometimes it is addressed, sometimes not. First, the analyst wants to know what function lateness serves. It may be observed for any length of time, without comment.

When working with self-destructive patients, how do we help them to turn the aggression out? In the treatment, we help patients to turn their rage and destructiveness into language directed toward us rather than toward themselves. Beyond that, since it is not the desire of analysts to be murdered or abused, we help the patients to discover methods of expression that will lead to greater fusion of destructive with constructive goals. Does the patient want to kill me for my crimes, or does he want to get some other form of satisfaction—for example, get me to behave better, or control me, or shut me up? If the patient is controlling, the analyst, instead of entering a battle for control, allows for control since it is better than a more regressed state where annihilation could be the only solution. Channeling destructive impulsiveness may be a result of the analyst's ability to accept the verbalization of previously unverbalized destructive impulses. One patient who was in a group said, "I could never put up with the people you do. You seem to enjoy it. Do you really like them?" Patients are sometimes amazed that the analyst puts up with them. When analysts are dealing with regression to preverbal times, a time of nuclear conflicts, it is important that they can be with these levels of impulse.

Just think of marriage. In marriage, one endures tension and excitation in the body. Divorce is sometimes the best available method for lowering the tension. Multiply the experience of marriage a hundredfold to get some picture of the involvement with a narcissistic patient. They sometimes see cutting or self-attack as the solution to their dilemmas. Of course, patients, too, are defended against these states. They may appear withdrawn, lacking any knowledge of their own feelings. Their defenses mimic results of the aging process in the general population. Pressures are too great. "All I want to do is get a farm and sit watching the grass grow." Age has a terrible effect on ego and energy. In the inexorable approach to death, the impetus to die gains a gradual foothold, and the impetus to live, to start new projects, diminishes. This is a return to the beginnings of life when babies can die in the crib if they are not coaxed into life by caretakers. It is easier to die than to live.

For Freud (1905b) and the early analysts, conflict was seen as this struggle between the internal push for the expression of drives and the external forces opposing that expression. In this view, mental health was the result of one's conscious decision to express or suppress different drives in accordance with the rules of society. When the sexual impulses were successfully repressed in latency, the theory went that the child was educable. When repression was not successful and impulses, pressing for discharge, returned, need for defense increased. Now we would say that in most emotional illness we do not see a struggle of impulse with defense but a struggle of one set of impulses against another. If the patient in the presence of the analyst is bottled up, overstimulated by internal states or by thoughts about the analyst's state, her body is suffering from overstimulation or an overexcitation that is too much for the body system to tolerate.

Under normal circumstances, options exist for dealing with overly tense states, such as intercourse or sexual discharge. If the patient has no outlet in the session for the quantities of excitation being bottled up, then the analyst joins the defense structure of the patient and, at the same time, seeks methods for controlling the stimulus level in the room. Even withdrawal or denial of feeling is better for the patient than the flooding and drowning of existing mental structures or, worse, somatic symptomatology.

What we mean when we speak of the patient as bottled up is that the patient experiences the energy level in his body as too intense. An agoraphobic patient is in a bottled-up condition in the transference when he suffers from having to leave the house to come to the analyst's office. He may limit the suffering by being accompanied by a certain person, driven in a car, or other means. The danger is experienced by him as external to himself. When he can be treated, we find that he is struggling with his own impulses, but they are seen as belonging to someone or something in the environment. So long as the patient can remain locked in the house, he does not suffer anxiety. It was patients like this who led analysts to an appreciation of the purpose of defense. Freud (1909a) did not think the anxiety avoided by phobia came from outside.

CHAPTER FOUR

~

Creating Psychic Change

Beginning the Treatment

Freud (1926) wrote that if a patient has a symptom, such as a hand-washing obsession, and she is prevented from carrying out the behavior, she will fall into a state of anxiety and regress. If the symptom developed in order to avoid an earlier outbreak of anxiety, it is puzzling why analysts for so long believed that informing the person of the meaning of this behavior would lead to its cessation and the end of anxiety. It was slow going as analysts studied the regressive results of the interpretive methods. It was not until ten years after Freud's death that Spotnitz (1969, 1985) developed his technical modifications of the interpretive technique, and analysts training with him began to move away from those interventions that attacked the patient's protective devices. Well into the eighties, practitioners in mental hospitals were being taught to acquaint patients, even psychotic patients, with the reality of their behavior. If we know that defenses prevent anxiety and regression and we recognize the danger in their premature removal, what interventions preserve the individual's integrity during analysis?

In an interview with Spotnitz several years ago (Meadow 1999), I asked him who he was. "You and Charles Brenner attended Harvard at the same time. You went to different medical schools, and you each returned to New York to study psychoanalysis at the New York Psychoanalytic Institute. You developed an interest in schizophrenia and wanted to treat it psychoanalytically. You presented a schizophrenic case for graduation and were told to present a different case. Brenner (1972), with Arlow, wrote about what was then the new ego analysis that came to dominate American psychoanalysis. You did not present another case but became a specialist in schizophrenia, a teacher, supervisor, and lecturer outside the mainstream. I understand that in 1949 you lectured to the American Psychiatric Association on your theory of emotional communication and exchanged letters with Winnicott on areas of agreement. Yet, outside the modern psychoanalytic school, your work was disregarded. Now contemporary analysts of other schools are beginning to arrive at ideas you introduced in the forties and fifties, including induced countertransference, bottled-up aggression, the use of narcissistic transference, and more recently the inefficacy of interpretation with preverbal material. However, you are rarely referenced in the classical literature when these discoveries are made."

In that interview, Spotnitz explained his lack of interest in a metatheory. He was interested in theory only to evaluate its usefulness in understanding the basic mechanisms present in psychopathology. He considered all the existing theories for their fit. In his first full-length volume, *Modern Psychoanalysis of the Schizophrenic Patient*, he reviewed the major conceptualizations and chose from each what his clinical findings validated. He thinks of himself as a researcher but is interested only in research that sheds light on what leads to change in psychopathology during treatment. He accepts Freud's (1923) theory of the biological base of drives. When asked questions about theory, he replies simply, "It's what works. It's what allows the patient to say everything."

In thinking about the goal of treatment, the goal of saying everything, one asks how each individual is created. Of what does his psyche consist? We know there is a somatic process. Edelman (1992) refers to the units in the nervous system that select and give different emphases to sensory experience and raises questions about how that selection process occurs. How do the selecting mechanisms relate to perception, categorization, and finally consciousness? What determines what we pay attention to? When we think of patients, we think of whether they seek sensory stimulation or try to avoid it. The sense of one's existence comes from categorizing experiences and making connections between them. We expect individuals to actively seek connections that satisfy basic needs. We don't believe that before birth the world is totally meaningless. People have selective attention and preferences in early infancy. There are innate biases and dispositions leading to patterns of moving, seeking, and staying alive. Values unfold (e.g., for warmth, for food, for control), and these values direct early strivings. Depending on their theories, analysts have called these preferences *instincts*, *drives, desires, wishes,* or *intentions.* Selection might be based on whether an object appears edible or inedible.

We know that before feelings there are reflexes. Among the innate mechanisms are detectors in the visual cortex of verticals, horizontals, boundaries, and angles—ways of conceptualizing the visual world. Infants use these mechanisms to make sense of the world and their internal stimuli. Edelman (1992) describes the process of creating objects as making maps by selecting those perceptions that offer help in explaining reality. Since, at an early stage, we do not store images of whole objects but store impressions in separate parts of the brain, the function of perception is to try to bring these together psychically. Edelman points out that this is not a process of seeing or controlling but one of constructing objects from color, shape, and movement. He points out that this activity precedes consciousness, concept formation, and attention.

With the advent of consciousness, one becomes aware of needs and feeling states or of longings, based on those needs. Does consciousness influence what we pay attention to? I assume the answer is no, so the first question I ask when a person consults me is *"Why?"* I may ask it aloud or study it silently. The patient may talk or remain relatively silent, but I am waiting to discover what is expected of me and the treatment. Am I the source of magic that will transform life, am I someone whom he wishes to work with to bring about some change, or what? When the analysand falls silent, I may ask a question or two, particularly if the silence appears uncomfortable. His counterforce to talking will stiffen if I am eager for him to talk. I may instead remain silent or talk myself. I want to study how he makes contact with me in order to define the demands inherent in his communications. My treatment begins with these observations on what my patient pays attention to.

With the new patient, I ask myself: Is he expecting me to perform magic. Is he interested in maintaining some dissatisfaction and repeating it? What is his real goal in coming here? I read between the lines to arrive at an understanding of that goal. I look for treatment destructive manifestations. I look for what I have to work with. While I am listening to why the patient is here, I am also looking for the patterns that he uses to separate himself. Is he going to be disappointed? Is he going to stay in the treatment with that disappointment, or is he going to leave? This is part of the silent analysis I do while the patient talks. He may present a new symptom. All the while I am looking for indications of bottled-up tension. It could be the constriction of a muscle, a tic. I follow the contact function of the patient, aiming not to overstimulate him. The bottling up I refer to is a biological phenomenon expressing itself in tension buildup and tension discharge. The body fills with tension when the patient does not have adequate discharge patterns for internal and external stimulation. One of the symptoms I may see is that he comes late to the sessions or he is unable to leave at the end of the session, lingering, unable to leave the room. If he jumps up and down on the couch, I understand that the stimulation he is experiencing does not have psychic outlets. Instead of thoughts about his discomfort, he moves to indicate the high level of tension he experiences. What we aim to do in treatment when we see this pattern is to resolve the patient's resistance to talking so that he can develop mental equivalents to these body actions. I am learning how much stimulation the patient can take, both in the room with me and in the world. I am learning how much of the tension originates in the interior and how much through the sensorium. Behaviors revealing a tension state take precedence when they appear in the session.

When a patient is silent, he may be comfortable, or he may be uncomfortable. He may want to punish the analyst; he may be testing the analyst. The analyst is interested in the motive for the silence. That will shape the intervention. I am also listening to increase my understanding of the core difficulties of the patient's adjustment.

We discover that analysands have odd ways of perceiving their experiences. Whatever they are, the analyst accepts and preserves these perceptions until the patient can entertain new ways of perceiving. Undifferentiated ego-object percepts will, in this approach, become highly charged with emotion. Only then do we deal with them as resistances. Immature, primitive behaviors arise following the instruction to talk. Spotnitz (1969, 1985) observed that these behaviors were more than resistances. They were also nonverbal messages. He refers to them as survival devices that should be respected as such.

Spotnitz (1969, 1985) called the fragmented ego as seen in schizophrenia the *narcissistic defense*. Freud (1916–1917b) said of narcissism that when treating it, "we come up against a wall which brings us to a stop." If the patient is blocking destructive action that would lead to further fragmentation, the analyst maintains the narcissistic defense as needed. We have learned that interpretation of defenses can cause narcissistic injury. If the patient is silent, that silence should be joined with no pressure to talk. Sooner or later the patient will make contact, and reflection by the analyst of his contacts will activate a narcissistic type of transference. In this transference, the patient molds the analyst's image to his own. Narcissistic transference appears positive, but when he sees the analyst as like himself, he can learn to love and hate the same object. He can learn to hate the analyst as much as he hates himself. One aims for discharge verbally of as much of the hostility as the partners in treatment can take. The analyst is neither neutral nor distant while working on narcissism. He can be gratifying only up to the point of not shattering the analysand's defense.

Modern treatment pays attention first to those patterns that would cause a break in the treatment. The danger is seen when the patient develops a new symptom, destructive impulsivity, or the stiffening of the narcissistic defense. This is the moment at which it becomes necessary to help him verbalize any hostility in as forceful as possible a way. Spotnitz (1969, 1985) called attention to other patterns that indicate a bottling up of tension: sudden extremes of tardiness, refusal to leave the room at the end of a session, jumping off the couch. In these cases a passive position adopted by the analyst could lead to the end of treatment. Even when the patient is oblivious to the action, the analyst brings it up.

While observing this, I will want a contract. When a patient is interviewed, I form an impression of how it would be to work with him. I either have a sliding or fixed fee for my time. I may prefer to work weekly, biweekly, or more often. If the patient has a preference and it fits with mine, I may decide to undertake treatment, set a fee, and arrange a frequency of sessions. The patient may say I would like to come five times a week and pay $5 per session. I may want $50 an hour and prefer to work with him once weekly. I am already in a discrepant situation. This is the potential patient's first demand. "Treat me as often as possible for as low a fee as possible." My answer is "Come as little as possible, work hard, and pay my fee."

One of the first lessons taught in analytic training is that if the analyst and another person agree to work together, a time, place, and fee must be agreed upon, and the conditions must be agreeable for the analyst and tolerable for the patient. I learned that the hard way. One case taught me the value of an agreeable treatment fee.

At twenty years old, Joan wanted to be an actress. She knew that to do this she had to leave her upstate home and travel to New York City. On her twentieth birthday, she told her mother she was leaving for the big city to find her destiny. She showed her mother an advertisement for an apartment to share and asked her for bus fare. She had written to a woman looking for a baby-sitter, so she could earn enough to pay for singing lessons, rent, and meals. A month later she was in my office telling me, "I don't know how you can help me. It would help if you could get me an audition or pay for my sessions, but I guess you don't want to do that." She concluded by saying, "I can't pay more than $5." This was Joan at her most talkative. She was one of my first patients at the treatment service, so I assured her that the fee was fine. Over the next few years she was prim and proper during sessions. She arranged her skirt neatly at her sides as the session began. She pressed her hair back and flattened it. She spoke in a monotone telling me the events of her day. Usually she complained about some treatment she had received that was either abusive or unthinking. It was difficult to discover how what she reported affected her because of the flatness of her tone. She rarely discussed her thoughts and feelings directly.

During the early treatment, Joan learned to take care of herself. Unironed skirts and blouses were now starched and pressed. She did not learn to think that she might be standing in the way of her own success. Some outside force was the culprit. She told endless stories about how other people were at fault for whatever happened to her. This was not to change as treatment progressed. Occasionally, I made what I called an "emotional communication," and they often reached her. One was the day I told her how cold she was. She brightened immediately and said, "That is exactly how I see you! I didn't want to tell you, but you seem emotionless. At this moment you feel much more real to me than you ever have."

There was truth in this response to my communication. Aside from my behavior as a reflection of hers, there was a resentment that had built in me as my practice grew, and feeling it was hopeless to think of raising her fee, I had not discussed it. She had moved on to a career in teaching and partially given up her ambition to act.

In her case, the insistence on entitlement should have given me the clue. She was not ready to give up dissatisfaction. Her insistence that she be taken care of would now alert me to her need for the status quo. This is a phase in treatment in which the analyst deals with the analysand's inertia or lack of interest in change. Usually the patient in the status quo phase acts like a 'good patient'. There is little presentation of problems. They are concealed in favor of appearing OK.

In the beginning of treatment, as I observe the contacts made to me by the analysand, I study another factor, the individual's tolerance for stimulation from both external and internal sources. How much the analyst talks during this phase is a function of the patient's style of contacting the analyst. For some people silence is ideal; for others it is overstimulating. So, too, is the offer of explanations of character.

An early goal is to study how to build the therapeutic relationship. Most psychotherapists would agree that consciousness is all we can know. Consciousness is usually described as the state during which one develops a sense that one exists and who one is. It is the point at which one can believe or sense that the experiences occurring now belong to "me." Once having experienced that, one can become aware of what happened before and can fantasize about what may happen in the future. It is this ownership of one's experiences that creates mind. The period of reflexive responses ends when one can have self-directed responses. Using a conscious model of treatment based on conscious wishes and intentions may lead to neglect of unconscious fantasies, fears, and desires.

I worry that if analysts ignore unconscious motives, those motives will control action without their knowledge and defeat the aims of treatment. Training in counseling and most forms of psychotherapy focuses on understanding the individual's conscious wishes. With what we now know about the brain, it seems pointless to ignore the strong emotions originating in the limbic or alligator brain and connected to our sensory systems, which, remote from conscious intention, influence behavior. We know the brain devises specific emotional patterns with which to respond to stimuli. This is not the creation of higher-order feelings but of the emotional states that modify both body and mind to form the substrate of our ability to feel deeply. Emotions cause physiological manifestations, such as changes in heart rate, as the brain registers internal shifts. We know of changes through images that are formed in the perceptual system or sometimes only recorded in the musculature. What can we know without knowledge of these out-of-consciousness processes? Can we know what we want? What will be missed in life if we do not take these processes into account?

If as psychoanalysts we ignore the unconscious, how will it influence the direction our treatments will take? How will actions dictated by the unconscious proceed, outside awareness, to carry patients away from fulfillment of their potential?

I doubt that anyone will deny what we now know about the functioning of the brain—that strong emotions arise from the deep recesses of the brain to direct behavior even when they have not entered consciousness. As practitioners we may raise the questions: Is analysis necessary? Do our analysands need to know their unconscious? Would analysis of consciousness suffice? Should the patient be referred elsewhere? I leave them for the reader to contemplate.

Throughout early treatment I am still observing. Is the patient hopeful and eager to learn about himself? Is he hopeless, seeking little encouragement from the outside? It is to answer these questions that, when beginning a treatment, diagnosis is important to the analyst. With these thoughts I shape my diagnosis. If I am to treat him analytically, I eventually want the patient to experience desire in the transference, but the timing is based on the extent to which he can tolerate arousal. Lost desires will surface in the treatment, but I try to remember that I am the guardian at the gate: neither too much nor too little.

"Mixing memory with desire" is done "live" in the treatment, and it is a tricky business. "Wanting to make progress" is the enemy of the beginning analyst. Ego insulation should take precedence over change.

It is not my job to provide information to the patient on how he defends himself. Intellectual understanding can interfere with emotional growth. I leave those interpretations to the ego analysts. We have learned that intellectual knowledge will not, over the course of treatment, lead to self-knowledge. It usually causes the patient to dig his heels in.

So, how is the analyst spending time in the sessions? Self-awareness on the part of the analyst is a major contributor to the success of treatment. Understanding the thoughts and feelings that result from being with a particular analysand requires the courage to face primitive residues in one's own personality. Thoughts and feelings we have can put us in touch with the experiences of the analysand and so can be used to serve the treatment. It is in this domain that the analyst thinks through her own goals and resistance to being where the patient is. Uncomfortable thoughts and feelings warn us that we do not want to go to places the analysand's pathology may take us. Part of the analytic work is reaching into our own unconscious inductions, and for this purpose, we use the patient as the analyst. Our own thoughts and feelings require exploration. Spotnitz referred to this in our interview, when I asked how he uses the patient for this purpose (Meadow 1999). His response was:

> [The patient] is telling you the way to go. He's arousing in you thoughts and feelings that have to be brought into analysis. You have to say to him, "I'm worried about this. I'm worried about that." After five years, an analyst can ask the patient anything. Any thought the analyst has about the patient, any concern, can be asked of the patient. Consult him. Use your patient as your supervisor in curing him, that is, if he wants to get well. Does he want to get well or does he want to die? (15)

Spotnitz added that if the patient wants to get well, he will lead you to your next question. Spotnitz voiced that he may respond with a negative therapeutic reaction: "You can't help me." As the analyst you will want to pursue that. "But do you want to help me to help you?" The patient has to learn to talk from the unconscious. When he does that, he tells you the story of the Other. If the patient says, "I don't know," he is told to say whatever comes to mind. It is his task to state the unconscious fully. It is not necessary that he understand what is said. In this process the core conflict reaches the cognitive level through the emotional experience of talking. New structures arise through this process. Through symbolic realization the patient discovers new feelings in the transference.

I served on a panel with an analyst who chose, for her presentation, the case I supervised. She described an affectless patient with fantasy monsters that she understood to express his vision of himself. They were slothful giants, asleep, unable to find the energy to wake. His life was devoid of meaning, vitality, and enjoyable relations.

The presentation was her first of this kind, and her wish was to give a brilliant presentation at the conference, but before the presentation she experienced some anxiety. In the presentation she described four years working with this man whose only contact was to report events and wait for a sign of approval. The patient had begun to be dissatisfied with his progress, and she was getting the same feelings. When she reported this in supervision, it seemed clear that the patient was making small movements away from passivity, but she was concerned that she might not be doing enough for his progress. That feeling got in the way of allowing the patient to continue to explore his dissatisfaction with where the treatment was, so that he could move to the active position of stating what he wanted. I believe it was the combination of her dissatisfaction with his progress and her wish to show her talent at the conference that led to her decision to present a more gratifying approach to the patient than the agreed-upon treatment plan to continue to work on the negative. She reported helping him with his expressed desire to remember the links between sessions. He reported that he felt gratified and offered new material in the sessions. This seemed to be progress, but it circumvented the core problem of his passivity.

In schizophrenia the nuclear problem is a powerful negative emotional charge. Hatred must be unmasked and directed outward in the treatment partnership. In neuroses problems are rooted in painful sexual ideas. If the passivity of the patient described earlier disguises his negative impulses, focus must remain on the negative.

With schizophrenics, treatment can move from such symptoms as hypochondria, depersonalization, delusion, and emptiness, from the withdrawal of narcissism to connectedness. Affection, love, kindness, and active assistance do not overcome the need for passivity. When the aforementioned patient began to express dissatisfaction, he demonstrated that he could for moments glimpse the analyst as a separate person. He could decide it was all right to say no. If he could be helped to fully enter the ambivalent stage, he would be conflicted between desire to abandon hope and desire for a connection. This is where I hope the supervisee can go with this patient. In this phase, a patient learns to lose and regain contact with objects outside his mind. I have observed cases as serious as catatonia in which this conflict is actively present. In the withdrawn catatonic, when a doctor or other contact person passes, the patient's frozen postures shift slightly. I have seen mannerisms and the emission of sounds similar to the mimetic noises of infancy as a patient moves toward object attachments.

In early modern training, students of analysis often believe that the discharge of rage and hostility will cure the pent-up personality. Later, they learn that discharge may be required at certain times but that discharge does not cure. In many cases, the repeated pleasure in discharge will increase the bottled-up condition. The important lesson is that motivation for change is a necessary concomitant. When this is present, the analysand can witness himself in the discharge process and can use it for life-enhancing purposes. When this motivation for change is missing, discharge of destructiveness is not the answer. Where motivation is present, finding a new outlet for discharge may be required to replace earlier pathways.

Prior to the development of the motivation for change, the technical approach depends on how serious the overload of stimulation is for the patient's psyche. The optimal level of tension for the session must be found, and this requires special techniques. In balancing the quantity of tension present, the analyst uses as a guide the rule that it should be below the level that would result in a somatic or psychotic regression. The analyst's first concern is that destruction not be directed to the body. Given that, in schizophrenia, attacks on the mind need attention. Finally, resolving destructiveness turned against the self can be worked through.

Strengthening the patient's desire to be well is a longer-term goal. New directions for discharge can be sought on a trial-and-error basis.

Regression to the preverbal defenses is seen in a number of pathological conditions. Among them are severe depression, hypochondriasis, psychosomatic disorders, and some of the severe neuroses. When considering appropriate interventions, one should understand that attention to symptoms is a detour. Verbal release of hostility should be handled first. It should be remembered, though, that careful handling of the negative in the treatment will not always lead to a cure of the narcissistic defense. Patients may cleverly conceal the dissatisfaction as it relates to the analyst. A technique that helps is knowing the unconscious meaning of each question the analysand presents during the treatment. An answer, without this knowledge, serves as a response to a false clue. The major problem in this is that an explanation offered will not work if it provides an unknown pathological gratification. To drain off the pattern of gratification in the pathology, a response by the analyst should be based on a genuine emotion experienced at the moment. One has given the correct intervention if the patient can talk meaningfully about himself immediately afterwards. He cannot do this when the pathological gratification is operating. Rather than trying to be the nourishing mother, I concentrate on how the individual handles his destructive impulses as they are mobilized in his mental apparatus during the contacts with me. Whether these impulses result from gratification, frustration, or a combination, the analysand needs a pathway for discharge of the bottled-up emotion that otherwise has the potential to push him into the schizophrenic response. As mentioned earlier, we guard against the most pathological patterns of discharge during sessions, those patterns that pour the tension into the body and can lead to somatic illness, those that lead to schizophrenic mental confusion, and those in which tension is turned against the ego and can lead to severe depressions.

Depression has taught analysts that Freud's (1917) theory on mourning is as important as his findings on anxiety. Anxiety theory was that frustrated libido was converted to anxiety. This theory ignores the loss of the object and the resulting inability to expect any kind of gratification. We find that although anxiety accompanies the unpleasure from any unfulfilled impulses, drive satisfaction alternates with the feelings resulting from object loss. Green (1999) predicted that we would recognize the significance of mourning in narcissism. He finds that "a specific transformation of affect is identification" and has written about the relevance of identification in the treatment of narcissism.

When the analyst understands a pattern, it is first analyzed silently, using one or more joining techniques. The analyst may reflect the analysand's expressions of low self-esteem. This kind of reflection is expected to reverse the flow of mobilized aggression from the self to an external transference object. In the beginning of treatment, it is undesirable to low-rate the analyst. It is only after the analysand has some feelings for the analyst as an external object that "low rating of the analyst" will help in the discharge of hostility (Spotnitz, 1969, 1985). For modern analysts, there is no standard theory of what will work, but it is believed that interpretation will be an important part of working through as the narcissistic defense is outgrown. When oscillating narcissistic and object-related transference states are observed, this process can begin, but working through cannot be considered a discrete operation. It applies to each resistance as it is resolved.

Analysts have discovered that standard interpretations given to a patient operating within the narcissistic defense can be mortifying and cause an increase in defensiveness. Interpretations are successful when the resistance of motivation to change is resolved and the analysand communicates in adult language. The only exception to this guideline is when an interpretation will improve immediate functioning in sessions. It is preferable to use emotional communications because they help the analysand to verbalize his own ideas. Questions that are reflected lead a patient to think of his own answers. Interpretation of unconscious mechanisms begins during the second year of treatment if motivation has developed for self-understanding and after emotional communications have weakened defective identifications. It is after these early treatment accomplishments that oedipal problems can be dealt with. Again, interpretations can be given by the analyst, but better results are obtained when answers emerge in the transference. In a training analysis explanations may be given of how resistance patterns were resolved according to the analysand's readiness to receive information.

Spotnitz (1969, 1985) described termination as a stage of stabilizing the gains made in early treatment. It is a period when new methods of dealing with impulses and dissatisfactions are used intentionally in preference to old ones. He believes that in the severely pathological personality this phase is very much like that of the oedipal patient. The difference is that there is a feeding back of induced feelings aroused earlier in the treatment (see Spotnitz 1976 on the toxoid response). The cure has been achieved when the patient has learned to behave appropriately without having to shut out feelings. This becomes possible because the patient has been equipped, throughout the treatment, with an abundance of action patterns that allow him to discharge all feelings. New feelings include the perception of self-fulfillment and happiness. They are demonstrated in an increased resiliency in abnormal situations. Retrospective analysis of narcissistic defenses dominate in the final months of a training analysis.

For modern analysts, treatment is based on a different concept than the one common in the traditional literature (i.e., defense as a protection against anxiety). Because affect and memory traces cannot be erased, defenses fail to solve long-range pathologies. As Spotnitz (1969, 1985) points out, defenses come into existence when needed to prevent damaging actions from occurring.

It took years for modern analysts to realize that traditional technique as practiced in America is radically different from Freud's technique. In a careful analysis of Freud, Sternbach (1990) notes the "unanalytic interventions" attributed to Freud, "particularly his deviations from the prescribed passive attitude of the analyst." Critics designated these as Freud's technical mistakes. They criticized his treatment of the Rat Man (Freud, 1909b) as "unanalytic." Quoting Lipton (1977), Sternbach (1990) writes that "the Rat Man is representative of Freud's mature work. . . . Since he lived another thirty years beyond and never changed his technique, it should be considered his definitive technique" (150). Freud (1912a, 1915b, 1916–1917d) always emphasized the use of the power of transference as the core of his technique. The flurry of classical papers criticizing Freud followed publication by Franz Alexander (1950) of his opposition to the classical emphasis on insight-oriented techniques. Alexander introduced the corrective emotional experience in analysis and attributed its success to the personality of the analyst. The criticisms were part of the attempt by classical analysis to make neutrality and opaqueness technical requirements of treatment, but, as Sternbach (1990) said, that approach is potentially harmful, leading the patient to narcissism by strengthening intellectualization.

Tracing Freud's (1913, 1914c, 1915b) technique further, Sternbach (1990) discovered that even when he used the word insight, it was not in the cognitive sense. Freud (1916–1917d) wrote that results rest upon "suggestion in the shape of transference." In "The Dynamics of Transference," Freud (1912a) described a "struggle between the doctor and the patient, between intellect and instinctual life, between understanding and seeking to act . . . played out almost exclusively in the phenomena of transference" (180). Responding to the misunderstanding of his techniques, Freud wrote two papers (1937a, 1937b) attempting to put the record straight, and his final statement was presented in the "Outline of Psychoanalysis" (1940).

What Do Patients Want from Analysis?

Historically, the medical model has not dealt with the kinds of issues psychoanalysts address. What might have happened if medical researchers had faced the unconscious fears that shape their research? In a delightful volume on the missing unconscious, Pollack (1999) examines the initial success of antibiotics, but the failure of medicine to note the fact that microbes, like the rest of living matter, are subject to mutations and thus by the laws of selection become resistant to antibiotics. The result is a serious disturbance in the natural balance between the immune system and microbes, with a resulting destabilization of the immune system. Now, as the fight against disease continues, we are confronted with new forms of the enemy we helped to change. It sounds like nuclear war. As medicine continues to fight each new microbe, inventing yet another antibiotic to deal with each specific variation (mutant), with the goal of beating the microbes into total submission, we ask, Would their domestication enable the immune system to coexist with the body's invaders? Should we assume that fear of the invader is the unconscious motive for this maladaptive approach to disease? If the answer is yes, what is it that is feared by the invasion of microbes? Is it the danger of loss of control of the boundaries that distinguish me from the rest of the world?

From work with schizophrenic patients, we have learned something of the deep fear both analyst and analysand may experience when confronted with the possibility of entering unfamiliar territory. In the late treatment of severe pathologies, the major resistances requiring attention are anxieties about new experiences. The analysand is inhibited in saying what he really thinks or feels and instead asks for rules to avoid meaningful communication. Still later, he can follow instructions but reacts negatively to taking responsibility for change. Spotnitz (1976) has explained this as a paucity or defect in identification patterns. He thought that group therapy could be helpful at this stage.

The death drive and the fear of death and loss present the greatest problem to medicine and to psychoanalysis. Analysts trained in medicine, if they deny knowledge of the desire to die, may work to clone their ideal image of the whole man. In the practice of medicine, we have seen science ignore the effects of aging and the needs of the dying in favor of dreams of eternal life. Medical journals read like a myth on endless life. Each report of a new medical breakthrough, the defeat of a particular germ, or the total eradication of a tumor leads to feelings of immortality that can last until the next difficulty appears. Nature has created us as mortals, but our unconscious clings to the fantasy that we will one day escape death.

Pollack (1999) asks of scientists, if the unconscious fantasy of omnipotence were not blocking them, could they concentrate on the real problems of living? For medicine, real problems might mean the chronic malignancies connected with aging and infectious disease. It could mean working to delay the aging process to lengthen life, slow the microbes to a crawl, and prevent cancer by reducing the external sources of DNA change to their barest minimum. In psychoanalysis as in medicine, we convince ourselves that conscious longings are enough. After all, our germ cells promise a kind of immortality. The union of sperm and egg promises eternity. Working to lengthen life has taken a backseat to the promise of eternity. When we consciously strive for the right man, baby, or, for men, the receptive woman, these wishes go to the heart of our unconscious longings. They have roots in the hard facts of biology.

Medicine and perhaps psychoanalysis are sometimes fooled into providing us with the wrong model. Take the sense of smell. We know that the brain is insensitive to odors but can respond to electrical signals from the olfactory centers by firing a signal that alerts us that something has been smelled. The signal may turn the clock back to a memory trace during embryonic development, even as early as the fertilization of the egg by sperm or perhaps to our own individual creation. Because babies have the power to process smell when they begin to breathe, they can hardwire each distinct odor to a particular part of the brain. Because there is no direct correlation between a region of olfaction and a region of the brain, because we cannot encode separate pathways to the brain for ten million olfactory receptors, this, what Pollack (1999) calls a distortion of the internal time clock, must follow each sniff or taste of the world and each time transport us back to when the body was first formed.

This process makes the world we can know through smell a peculiar part of all the possible worlds each of us can know. Each of us is limited by early acquisitions of specific smells. I have often thought when asked whether I do telephone sessions that I do not want to because sensory impressions, like the sense of smell, are so important in arousing affects. We know that regression to the time of fertilization can result in an odor secreted by the egg cell, which is capable of a change in the direction of the sperm tail propeller that helps the sperm find its way to the egg. Is the protein smell produced when the drive for fertilization is strong? What causes a man to be responsive to a woman? Do men want to give a woman what she wants when she has the right smell? Is it a fact that postmenopausal women do not arouse men because of these unconscious connections? Older men and women walk around acting as though they are still in the game. Are they acting on memory?

Other smells return us to the construction of a part of the brain and can take us to the very beginning of our individual existence. Does each of us want on the deepest unconscious level to reexperience the beginning of that unique existence? Or is mating, fertilization, and producing offspring sufficient?

Working as an analyst, I've learned that humans seem to want something they cannot have, but at least they want to achieve a survivable balance within themselves. I remember many years ago seeing a movie starring Susan Hayward, titled *I Want to Live*. In it Susan is on death row waiting to be executed for murder. Each morning she is taken from her cell to the dentist's office where the technician works meticulously in her mouth to repair cavities and to pull teeth. I wondered then why, if she is dying, are they doing this? It seems that most of us pretend until the last moment that life will go on forever. Most people want life to go on forever or, at least, to live as long as they can. Some qualify that wish with the addendum "as long as the comfort level does not drop too low." If we think that biology truly shapes what we want and some of these drive states do govern us, it is much easier to understand the fantasies and dreams that are reported in the course of each individual analysis, those fantasies that make no sense if we try to explain them in terms of consciously reported wishes.

In the beginning phase of treatment, we will not solve all the problems connected with deep unconscious fantasies, so I save that for another chapter. When beginning a treatment, reports of dreams are approached as any other material in the session. We ask ourselves, What does the patient want me to know?

Creating Psychic Change in Individual Analysis

Early in the nineteenth century, in what was called the topographical phase of psychoanalysis, the method of analysis was interpretation of unconscious forces and affects. Analysts wanted to make conscious what was unconscious. Specifically, they were interested in the contents of the repressed unconscious. Seeking the repressed unconscious required acceptance of two assumptions: (1) What is repressed is representations of unacceptable drives, and (2) the reasons for rejecting urges can be discovered in a reconstruction of the patient's early childhood experiences.[1]

Freud's (1924) later work on masochism and narcissism led him, by 1923, to a theory of mental structures. As he suggested in "The Ego and the Id" (1923), the psychic structure consists of specific systems—an id, an ego, and a superego, each performing specific functions. Whether the contents of the psyche were conscious or unconscious lost its central place in analytic thinking. But insights into the mobility of psychic energy created new problems. It was clear that drive discharge was more significant than the object used for discharge. Objects could be replaced by others that would provide more satisfaction. Not only was the object replaced by another in the search for drive discharge, but one aim could be substituted for another. This left analysts with a contradiction between the mobility of energy systems and fixed structures. We have seen results in the psychoanalytic literature of the search for an integrating structure—an unconscious ego—as the controlling force in behavior. One unfortunate outcome of this development, at least to drive-oriented psychoanalysts, has been the approach based on a hermeneutic story line grounded in wishes and intentions. It gave up the search for underlying causes because this new route offered a science of observation, moving away from inferences of the earlier theory of connection to childhood trauma. On the other side, it gave analysts a way to work with patients toward explanations that could be acceptable by both. It failed in that it did not bring about change.

For the four or five decades following the emergence of structural theory, the search for integrating principles in the unconscious occupied much of the thinking and writing of psychoanalysts. It was assumed that unconscious fantasy could only exist after the development of language. Lacan (1977) built his whole theory on early Freud and on an unconscious structured like a language. Ego analysis replaced the search for unconscious meaning with repetitive behavior patterns—compromise formations condensing drive and defense. This approach seemed more scientific and less mythical than the belief in unconscious fantasies. The analyst observed and looked for organizing principles.

There is a problem stopping at conscious agreements between patient and analyst that the causes are known perceptions put into language. True, through observation of repetitive patterns we bring explanation out of chaos, but learning about the repressed unconscious does not help us to understand the deeper level—the primal unconscious—through which we can bring patients to a fuller appreciation of the self. To go beyond early childhood experiences to the "never conscious unconscious" requires traveling another path with patients, one in which they speak in tongues other than the verbal. Is this other level potentially capable of verbal organization? Can we reach it in full knowledge of the absence of language and structures in the depths of the psyche? Unconscious fantasy seems like an anomaly to many analysts, but I have found it useful to view unconscious fantasy as a preverbal container in which the helpless infant conducts his first search for discharge of endogenous drives. We see this in the powerful emotional experiences we have with music and poetry that can touch universal levels of human experience without our awareness of just what the basis is for our response.

The Case of Don

I treat a man in group as well as in individual treatment. This man always says, "I don't want to be involved in anything." To his wife, who is an administrator in an analytic institute, he says, "I don't want any jobs. Don't ask me to do anything." Following a major renovation at the psychoanalytic institute, this young man took on the responsibility for ordering and designing the placement of the telephone and computer lines. "I didn't want to," he told me, "but I didn't want to be left out there alone, so I signed on to arrange for the new lines for the building." In group analysis, he repetitively arouses anger, sometimes by seeming naïve, often by correcting the perceptions of group members through pointed questions. Each time a group member expresses exasperation with his behavior, he speaks of getting up and leaving or wanting to separate. Over the years he had isolated himself, but recently he has expressed a desire for contact. But when he moves toward contact, he repeats the provocative behaviors. When he decides to be a "family member," he acts helpless and dependent, asking, "What should I do with this? How should this be done?" His dependent statements also cause minor irritations in "the family." Why does he act as though the simplest task is too complicated for him? He has difficulty understanding what is upsetting group members when this happens. If he could accept the wish instead of enacting helplessness, he would not have to flee to isolation as his only alternative.

On one particular day several group members were complaining that the telephones were not working at the treatment institute. When an irate woman questioned him, he sounded very innocent. He had agreed to contact the phone company and leave a diagram with the contractors. That was all! His job was finished. When asked if he meant to enrage her, he burst out emotionally, exclaiming that this is why he can't stand being in a family. Families are toxic. Every time he allows himself to get close, the other family members try to kill him. His fantasy of being alone and away from the family involves thoughts of writing great works of literature and being very successful. When he isolates himself and tries to write, he feels overstimulated. When his editors want to help him and push him to keep at it, the desire to stop work is aroused. As a child he was sent to a boarding school in another country, but he had no conscious fantasies of why the family sent him away. On the object level, the fantasy is that involvement with a family means submission and loss of self, not the passive place he longs for. He says angrily, "People are always trying to get me to do something." He does not intend to be ordered around or made to do other people's bidding. They won't let him lie back and do nothing. This man's conflict between connection and disconnection can be related to issues of rearing and to feelings of pressure and discomfort, but can we tease out what ties him to the need to get away from the pressures of relating and repetitively recreating the same experience with objects? Why does he cling to the image of himself as "unwanted and unlovable" and ignore the power of his death instinct?

Tracing this man's attraction to life as it interacts with his desire to escape pressure is difficult within the model of an id that seeks discharge for drives and an ego that erects countercathexes to block drives. If we shift to a model in which drives work cooperatively with each other for discharge or oppose each other in pathological adjustments, we can explain this man's conflict around getting connected or not being connected in his response to connecting the telephones.

I can better understand what will cure this man if I consider his temperament—a passive orientation and longing for low tension levels within his body. If his dealings with the world were not created solely by his experiences in the family—his denial of rejection in the family—what do I next examine? It is true that I can track other behavior to early experiences in his history in the family—for example, his feeding patterns. In the first few months of life, his reaction to being fed was rage and withdrawal. His mother had followed the medical advice of the period, feeding him on a rigid time schedule. She told him later that she cried when she heard his screams but stuck to the plan. The hyperirritation he experienced paralleled an earlier experience with birth. His mother, having had two easy deliveries, expected the birth to take two or three hours, but this child didn't seem to want to leave the uterus. After thirty hours of labor, he was finally delivered by forceps. Another fact from his preverbal life was the development of asthma at eighteen months. A repetitive feeling that he was suffocating finally shaped itself into this physical symptom. Many questions occur when thinking about the formation of his character. Did he struggle in the intrauterine period with boundaries that limit the body's activities? Did he have body knowledge of the space that he occupied?[2]

In the transference were many reports of his attraction to passivity, even death. He reported gagging and vomiting in response to dentists opening his mouth and similar reactions, such as difficulties breathing, in other bodily invasions. He experiences himself as drawn to death or, at the very least, isolation whenever life is too much for him, as when the editors overstimulate him by coaxing him to perform. When, during a group session, I said to him emotionally, "I am going to send you to Florida," he was overcome with rage and the feeling that he wanted to run out of the room. This time, instead of running, he experienced the intensity of the urge. When I said, "We don't have to go on with this now," the thought occurred to him that no one was really to blame—that he had always struggled against the stimulation of the life force.

Is it worthwhile to dwell on the innate balance between two sets of drives that, in their specific balance, could be said to define the individual? In this man I infer a stronger pull toward lower tension levels than a verve for life. It was present from birth through early infancy into adult life. What I have noticed in the transference is that as he learns more of his true nature, he moves toward more connection. The passivity in his character, while always present, interacts in a new rhythm with the life force.

Piontelli's (1992) work with fraternal twins is relevant here. In her study of the fraternal twins Marc and Celia, she observed that Marc, *in utero*, was slow to turn, buried himself in the placenta, and made no contact with his twin. Celia, on the other hand, bounced, examined her toes and fingers, touched Marc, and, in general, exhibited interest in the surround. How can this information be used? After birth, it was observed that the mother seemed to favor Marc. She attended to the unresponsive child, put the breast to his mouth, sang to him, and rocked him. When the exuberant Celia played and made contact, she was pushed away and told to be quiet. The boy's character remained constant over the first eighteen months of his life outside the uterus. He did not develop an interest in life. Celia was different. She became depressed, giving up much of her lively behavior. It was clear that the mother's nurturing behavior with Marc did not change the balance between his drives, but with Celia it led to a style that hid her love of life.

As analysts, how can we use knowledge of temperament, for example, with the man whose stronger desire to disconnect conflicts with the weaker desire for connection? In treatment, will I work with my patient only to undo his denial of family rejection? What will I do with the dominance of passivity or the attraction to death in his personality? I surely cannot know fully the relative strength of constitution and personal experience, but if I am careful to follow the contact function of each patient during sessions, I will discover the role passivity now plays, and the patient will not experience an intolerable rise in tension level in his body during treatment, nor will he be exposed to my pet ideas. The contact function is a technical approach developed within modern psychoanalysis for the treatment of narcissism. The goal is to provide a "twin image" for the patient through reflection of his perceptions. Interpretation is kept to a minimum if it introduces thoughts or feelings outside the patient's awareness. This approach to treatment is maintained until and unless a patient actively seeks information.

Unconscious Fantasy

Arguments over whether there can be unconscious fantasy prior to language remind me of the struggle that ensued between the followers of Melanie Klein and Anna Freud, following Anna Freud's arrival in London in 1938, a debate over early object relationships. In their disagreements at the "Controversial Lectures" at the British Society in 1944–1945, the Klein group insisted that fantasy develops with the first instinctual urge. Ego analysts emphasized the need for an integrating unconscious psychic structure for the formation of imagery and affect. They argued for an unconscious ego. For many who emphasized resistance analysis, the baby, unconscious fantasy, got thrown out with the bathwater.

The question was: Could Klein's (1946) early object relations theory be compatible with Freudian drive theory? Anna Freud (1936b) said that the mother is essential, but the baby does not "know" this. Isaacs (1948) used as her argument for preverbal object relations the behavior observed in infants under one year of age. In play, the child hides things, gets rid of them, breaks them, sucks them. She presented these behaviors as evidence that the child is restoring the nipple to his mouth, bringing back the lost mother or sending her away or separating her from the father (Hayman 1989). But do these observed behaviors require a concept of "objects"? Moderns said that the explanation lies in Freud's (1926) theory of bottled-up tension seeking discharge where the exact cause of tension is not necessarily known by the infant. Working with narcissism has clarified for me that there is no object awareness in the first few months of life. Klein's (1946) claim that some form of fantasy exists from the very first urge the infant or fetus experiences has proved useful. In Freud's model, the infant seeks the experience of well-being or its opposite, unaware of any external source of the feeling state. Using the narcissistic solution is more economical than seeking imagery of a "self and other," a "me and not me" in this early state. Neither Kleinian early object theory nor ego analysis and structural constructs have improved on Freud's (1920) dual drive theory. Lacan's (1977) offer of the word as the instigator of unconscious fantasy is useful.

I cannot tell you how excited I was several years ago at a Harvard lecture by Brenner where he raised doubts about structural theory. At another lecture at the New York Psychoanalytic Institute, I was relieved to hear him say that "there is no part that is mature, integrated, and free of conflict as the structural theory assumes" (Brenner 1994: 3). In his presentation, however, the model of drive-seeking based on experiences with objects remained. It left us searching for "the calamities of childhood" as the root of conflict, one not clearly distinguished from a child's interpretation of what is happening within and around him. It provided no room for preverbal experiences of infancy and the intrauterine stage.

We can appreciate childhood influences and connect memories to specific patterns in the repetitions, but are they the cause of conflicts or only the top level? Making a connection between "now" and "childhood calamities" does not necessarily lead us to the deeper roots of conflict, the struggles between drive states locked in unresolved battles for dominance. I believe it is more parsimonious to think of the energy flow between two drive sets than of a mind divided into agencies. Brenner did not discard the whole structural package, but I believe he took a major step toward a theory of drive states or urges that utilize the perceptual apparatus to serve the endogenous need for discharge when he asserted that more constructs are *just not* necessary. In Brenner's (1991, 1994) recent writings, he has recognized that the assumptions of structural theory have *not* been demonstrated to be effective inferences in clinical observation. He has recognized that every thought and perception gratifies one or more drives at the same time. He has concluded that structural explanations may give an incorrect idea of what can be achieved in psychoanalysis, but he has raised questions about whether the disadvantages of a structural explanation are great enough to justify giving up structural theory. His solution to the treatment dilemma is to suggest that treatment can replace pathological compromise formations with normal compromises, by which I believe he means less pathological defenses.

If we believe that neither structural theory nor Klein's early object theory is parsimonious—if we agree with Freud (1905b) and Anna Freud (1954) that there is a period in the first few months of life when the individual is in an autoerotic phase, free of object images—why do we think of anything in this phase other than sensation? What can we say of mental representations and causes? Does character begin months later? Recent neurophysiological findings tell us, on the one hand, that fixed objects cannot be stored but are created in each drive arousal. On the other, the establishing of synaptic connections, resembling Freud's (1905a) somatic compliance, indicates a method of processing experience that can be called "primitive mental organization" somewhere between pure sensation and full fantasy.

When treating patients working through preverbal conflicts, an analyst is confronted with the somatic and with symptoms such as anxiety and panic, as well as the more direct enactments in the treatment relationship. As the patient develops a narcissistic transference, she tells us what she herself does not know. Feelings induced in the analyst tell us how the patient views herself and the world.

If we think of how one moves from primitive expressions to a linguistic form of expression, we must examine prefeeling, primitive fantasy states. If I have a patient who "thinks" with his body, I want to help him organize his experience in language accompanied by affect. Observing patients, the analyst learns what cannot be said and tries to replace "enactments and symptoms" with words. We believe a patient is cured when he can think and say everything. We believe his method of resolving conflicts when healthy will include getting in touch with the preverbal on the occasion of each drive arousal in order to understand the roots of these preverbal conflicts between the drives struggling for dominance. It is important that we not lose sight of the uniqueness of each person's internal balance of the forces of Eros and Thanatos.

Over time, analysts have relied on the reconstruction of childhood experience, deemphasizing how innate tendencies and experience shape character. We can appreciate the work of Peter and Alexander Neubauer (1996) because they have investigated genetic inheritance and produced clinical evidence for our belief that inherited qualities shape the way we use the world and how we perceive it. Life patterns that work for patients are based on temperament and innate tendencies. The Neubauers' work on maturation adds another dimension to the study of temperament by recognizing the variety and modes of its expression at each maturational level. For example, sensitivity or perceptiveness in early life may become shrewdness in the adult, or receptivity to touch may lead to a personality easily aroused. When life imposes on my patient who prefers low levels of tension, he will discharge along somatic paths or reject and isolate himself as he did in infancy. His breathing will become irregular when he is overstimulated. Breathing is his preverbal language. He will move, as he did in early asthma attacks, toward disconnection and death, and then, fearing death, respond with a sharp intake of air. Considering these prelanguage languages is valuable for the analyst who is interested in tracking the earliest mental developments in which inheritance dictates how experience will be shaped in the search for drive discharge. Observing patients, we learn how biology limits and at the same time creates our views of the world.

If we admit that the reconstruction of infantile trauma is not the only answer to why we are what we are, then how do we reconstruct what we are? I have found that when observing patients, it helps to remember that they are biological creatures responding to an environment with a unique balance between the tension-reducing and the constructive life-seeking drives. Two children of different temperaments placed in the family of childhood of my "connection" man could have very different life styles as outlets for their conflicts. Between biological discharge-seeking drives and learned experience, each individual uniquely creates him- or herself. We know that difficulties imposed by the environment are dealt with differently by children with different temperaments. Temperament affects what each child reacts to and what kinds of inner representational world he or she will create. The Neubauers in *Nature's Thumbprint* elucidate the difficulties that I saw in Alice, a patient of mine who was exposed to the "wrong move at the wrong time" when her parents relocated to a state distant from the friends she had grown up with. Alice felt alienated and empty at college and asked to live at home and go to a local college. When I saw her, it was evident that the current situation was provoking suicidal thoughts.

The compelling evidence of a repetition was revealed when Alice described a lonely adolescence in a new suburban community with no means of transportation while her parents were at work. She was isolated from other family members—uncles and a grandmother—when her family relocated from one state to another. She remembered standing by the moving van as the family prepared to leave their home, screaming that she would not go. She would not leave her school, her friends, her home. Within a few minutes, she had been loaded into the car and whisked away. The helpless feeling, the depression, and the eventual loneliness became the pattern of her adolescence. As a young child, she was conflicted about her femininity, her father's sadism, and her mother's phobias. She adopted a sarcastic tone and asserted a superiority over others, both in her demeanor and in her talk. This stance supported two wishes. She was right or superior—she did not have to tolerate confused mental states—and she was in charge. That is, she could with phobic determination limit stimulation from the environment. Her life with a younger woman allowed her to avoid the feelings of helplessness that she dreaded. The difficulties imposed by her environment combined with her individual makeup to cut her off from her loving feelings. She was in control of her life.

I realized that the move from the calamities of childhood to the concept of fused drive states is not such a great leap. If we consider life in energy terms, we think of the ebb and flow of tension buildup (striving) and tension reduction (withdrawal). This is certainly a model that more closely explains the observable data. And this does not preclude Brenner's (1982) idea that conflict remains active in healthy persons, but it does put a different spin on it. For each of us, the search for activities and enactments that lead to a fusion of these two tendencies is an ongoing struggle against the determination of the life and death forces to separate or exist in the defused state.

If analysts find the structural division of function too narrow with an id exclusively as the agency of drives and an ego as the agency of perception, they might entertain the idea that the fundamental purpose of perception is to seek the best routes to drive discharge. The perceiving individual scans internal and external possibilities much as an animal living on the plain scans the horizon for meat with increased motivation when hungry. He uses assertion; he uses his senses; he focuses; he does not lose track. With patients, we investigate how the two drive sets are mixed. Sternbach (1975), writing on this process, describes the pattern of the sexual orgasm. He saw the cooperation of Thanatos and Eros as a prototype for healthful activity.[3] He points out that coitus is characterized by a rhythmic approach and withdrawal of two bodies accompanied by an alternating increase and decrease of tension rather than as in the popular image of tension increase to the point of orgasm followed by a sharp drop in tension. He writes:

> Before the apex quantitatively large and rising increases of tension alternate with small and smaller decreases. This rhythm, in which tension increase is prevalent but not exclusive, is experienced as extremely pleasurable leading to

the subjective feeling of union. When the tension begins to cause pain, the driving force aiming at tension decrease overwhelms the binding forces and the rhythm changes. Rushing decreases of tension, but counteracted by alternating, now painful, but smaller and ever smaller increases of tension follow until tension is completely discharged and no further increase takes place. During the act, the action is carried by energies with opposite tendencies fused for one integrated aim, sexual ecstasy, combined with the highest degree of unity, followed by a reduction of tension and the desire to separate. (391)

I noticed that Brenner (2000) does not use the concept of fusion of drives, and I have wondered whether this is because of the difficulty of separating out its connection with the preverbal object so basic to Klein's ideas. The concept of fusion of drives only makes sense if we abandon drive/defense and replace it on the preverbal level with the model of drive fusion.

Heterosexual and homosexual acting out offer examples in which the patient has been able to connect the death drive to sexual satisfaction in an "apparent" fusion of life and death instincts. However, erotic energies merely seem to increase the violent tendencies. We were at first confused by the erotic tendencies until we recognized, case by case, how erotic tendencies were used to permit destructiveness to overpower constructive goals. In her early work, McDougall (1978) writes about the narcissistic lesions that lead to such fusions. The unconscious demand foisted upon the partner called upon to repair them gives a more compulsive and more destructive aspect to the exchange. I have asked myself: Did the concept of an unconscious ego in battle with an unconscious id get in the way of our understanding of the role of preverbal instinctual energy in the creation of character? Drive fusion does not mean the end of conflict. The search for fusion is a lifelong struggle fraught along the way with conflict.

Beginning in 1948 with the work of Hyman Spotnitz at the Jewish Board of Guardians, analysts began to integrate resistance analysis of drive derivatives with an analysis of the preverbal unconscious. Work with prefeelings and the early fantasy forms of communication led to insights into the way humans psychically experience their urges when drives oppose each other prior to the development of language. It was the study of fantasy and its formation that gave us information on drives in conflicts, an early innovation of modern psychoanalysis working with schizophrenics.

Psychic Change

If analysts had stayed with Freud, moving simply from his early economic theory to his later dual drive theory, it would have been a simple step to the concept that these energies may either struggle with each other for discharge, or they may find outlets that satisfy both. While the ego analysts moved to a model in which drives were met with countercathexes erected against drive discharge, the modern group moved to a model based on individual variations in patterns between these two energy fields.

Two problems developed for the ego analysts: First, an object relations model was needed to explain the defenses against drives, and, second, language was believed necessary to develop conflict and fantasy. This led eventually to a stalemate for ego analysis. It did not offer a methodology for the study of prelanguage functioning; instead, it got stuck looking for an unconscious ego. For moderns, other problems arose. If the balance between drive states varies from person to person according to genetics, constitution, and experience, how does the analyst work with a twin like Marc who is dominated by a desire for low tension levels? Fusion theory made it possible for modern analysts to think of the dynamics of psychoses and early infantile fixations. It expanded for us the range of cases that could be treated.

I treat a man who feels like a little boy surrounded by powerful women. His behavior can best be called the "head of the household" syndrome. In his family he knew what everyone should do. He held family meetings that reminded one of Marlon Brando playing the Don in *The Godfather*, yet, using an induced feeling, I asked, "Are you getting it up the ass again?" This both irritated him and made him laugh. His unconscious image of "loser" was touched by these interchanges. When a serious family problem arose in which he was summoned as the head of the family, rage and fantasies of vindictive action led him to the brink of harming the perpetrator.

The intervention that helped him was one he was just about ready for. I suggested that he admit to the family that he was helpless and could do nothing about the situation. He fought the idea but admitted the alternative was to do that or hire a killer. When he told his family how helpless he feels, they expressed relief. They were tired of playing the helpless role to his king. He, too, experienced relief. He told me he found it pleasant to face himself and not be afraid of who he really is. To mature, patients need to let go of their disguises. Knowing oneself at one's current state of maturation is a first step in the growth process.

When we examine conflicts between drives, we reach deep into unconscious fantasy to an archaic, preobject unconscious in which the interaction between the drives is as varied as the number of individuals on the planet. One difference working with the preverbal patient is that the earlier longings and motives relate to the dyad rather than to the triad of the oedipal phase. In narcissism, when a regressed patient is symbolically fed, he may create a blissful fantasy of a union with a wonderful internal "cause" of his pleasure, often experienced as the patient's own omnipotence. In narcissism, the search for union with another person can be seen as a longing for reconnection with a missing part of the self. It is a way of expressing the unconscious fantasy that one possesses an internal force that reduces drive tension, and the patient is frightened when it is lost. We can call these fantasies prefeeling states, or actions to control tension. They are a language for drives. Whether we call them unconscious fantasies, body conversions, or narcissistic objectless enactments, what we know is they are forms of communication closer to the biological level than to mental life. They can be thought of as the rhythms of life as in Sternbach's description of coitus.

Understanding what is meant by "unconscious fantasy" is no simple task. The literature does not define it clinically. After all, when fantasy can be stated, it is conscious fantasy. Drives can lead to grandiose fantasies of a heroic nature. "I can do anything; I am the master of my fate." These fantasies are related to the ability, or inability, to control drive discharge. What remains outside awareness is the purpose the fantasy fulfills. The study of art forms and aesthetics and the psychoanalysis of patients have come closest to revealing the character of unconscious fantasy. Artists will tell you that a fragment of an experience will lead them to a creative act. The scene seems to touch something outside their awareness from inside, and it becomes the core of the art form that unfolds. What is uniquely moving to each individual as he moves through his life resides in his unconscious. At different maturational levels, different contents have meaning as they arise to add to the shape of one's character.

Patients are arrested at one or another stage of development through developmental challenges from all the other phases that are still operable in their characters. A patient has just been able to tell me after many years of treatment that he feels safe with me. He claims that although I know how bad he is, I will not hurt him. He is only now beginning to talk about how destructive he believes he is when dealing with others. It is clear that he fears the intensity of his drives. He is starting to emerge out of isolation. Feeling connected to analysis has been a growing feeling in him. Feeling he will be abandoned means he can reveal more of himself. He can now say I have disappointed him. There are parts of him I don't know. "You don't know what it feels like to have two aces in your pocket," he exclaimed. I have asked him if he would like to give up chronic disappointment and be with someone who fully understands him. His answer, "I can't imagine it."

I asked whether he would help me to know the parts I don't know. However, he is not sure what he may be capable of doing. The secret behind his wall of detachment and isolation was a belief in his badness. Much as the phobic avoids certain situations, he avoids contacts that might lead to acting on impulses.

There is an unconscious, and it can be demonstrated to be the guiding force in the psychic development of an individual. Psychoanalysis is a unique method for uncovering fantasies of the preverbal level to arrive at the history of the individual's character formation.

Modern analysts study "enactments" within the transference as the royal road to preverbal life. Part of this approach is to understand somatic symptoms and fantasy formation as primitive mental phenomena designed to express preverbal conflicts. When analysts say there is no possibility of unconscious fantasy before language, they ignore the forms of language that precede the verbal, they ignore how we talk with our bodies and our actions—communications that must be regarded as psychic acts because they have direction.

For a modern analyst, part of the success in working with preverbal conflicts lies in the analyst's willingness to know his own unconscious. Spotnitz (Meadow 1999) noted that dreamers will frequently talk to the analyst directly from the unconscious through their dreams when the analyst's responses indicate an acceptance of unconscious fantasy. The analyst's induced feeling states tell him the "meaning" of dreams in the session.

Consider the following. In a transference dream, a patient is watching her mother-in-law die. In discussing the dream, she thought she was the person dying. I said, "When I last saw you, you were concerned about how I was doing. Is that me in the dream? Are you too nice a person to put me on the deathbed? You dream someone is dying who is already dead instead of you or me dying. Isn't that the choice, you or me?" She responded, "Yes, if the choice is you or me dead, I would rather kill someone already dead and be a nice person. It is not in my genes to say it's got to be you, not me. How can I change my character when I feel like killing myself?"

By viewing associations as defensive operations of the personality, analysts have studied how the patient leads an analyst away from core issues, distracting her with associations, taking her up to the level of conflicts between self and other. Brenner (1994) pointed out that even the manifest dream presented in analysis must be regarded as a first association to the "real" dream. When whatever comes up in the session is considered in the transference, it is possible to decipher the dream. We ask, Why this dream now? Why is it told to me?

Understanding the defensive function of dream associations has led analysts back to the proper business of analysis, that of defining the content of each individual's unconscious in its own peculiar uniqueness. The particular genetic and constitutional foundations and the unique personal experiences will be found in what the patient says and does not say, what he does and does not do in the presence of the analyst.

A question we must now answer is: What are the bases of therapeutic action? A modern psychoanalysis uses the narcissistic transference to uncover preverbal factors in psychic behavior. As the individual's narcissism fluctuates with object contact, childhood memory traces are used to confirm what is felt in the transference—those conflicts that live on in the personality.

Students in supervision remind us of the difficulty in learning to use the feeling level of the patient's communications. In a hospital internship, a supervisee reported a patient who talks of wanting to get out of the mental hospital. He wants to be free of schedules and nurses giving him meds.

ANALYST: Why does he want to get out of the hospital? Does he tell you? Will he be free if he gets out of the hospital? What will he be free of?
SUPERVISEE: He wants to be free of the nurses, the meds.
A: So he doesn't like these impositions from the outside. Does he ever talk about wanting to be dead, or is it just that he wants less pressure?
S: He has lots of fantasies. He wants to be a gangster so he can get anything he wants without paying for it.
A: So he wants an exciting life, free of restrictions, free of controls. Why a gangster?
S: So he can have anything he wants.
A: Why doesn't he want to be rich and be able to pay for it?
S: He thinks he will maybe be a rock star and have plenty of money.
A: This sounds like a very normal man to me. What got in his way? How did he get himself committed?
S: Well, he assaults people.
A: Oh, so he can't control his impulses. Is that what he's talking about? If he wants to get what he wants, how come he goes around assaulting people, getting himself locked up and having all these nurses to contend with? Could it be that on some level, there's something appealing about having nurses control him. If he got out of the hospital, he would have to control himself.

The analyst need not, nor should not, provide an interpretation of this patient's desire for freedom. If we accept the patient's perception of his situation, using emotional induction to enter the patient's fantasy, the patient who feels trapped will learn that the pain comes from inside. When these feelings are structured in language in the presence of the analyst, more sophisticated fantasies develop out of the creative processes within the patient. As Brenner (1994) has suggested, the analytic process can move the patient from pathological defenses, as in projection and denial, to a recognition of his pain as part of an internal process.

A candidate-in-training at one of the analytic training institutes demonstrated that taking a first step with a patient opened up a whole new realm in his own character. During his first year in supervision, he despaired because his patient was repetitively troubled by a fear that she would become schizophrenic and end up in a mental hospital as her mother had. This fear persisted into the following year and did not respond to his supportive or interpretive interventions. I suggested that he tell her she had nothing to worry about. In all probability she was already schizophrenic but was living outside a hospital. The supervisee was horrified. "I could never say that to a patient," he said. "It would be unethical." We had this interchange over time until finally he suggested that if he was not going to try anything I suggested, perhaps there was nothing to learn here. I agreed. When confronted with the freedom to leave without trying a joining technique, the supervisee decided he would try it once to see what effect it had but would surely tell her it was not true if she seemed disturbed. He made an intervention to her that was even stronger than the one suggested. "You are already schizophrenic!" he announced. He was surprised at her calm and at the new material she produced connected with her fear. After she had left the session, he looked out the window and observed her clicking her heels in the air in leaps of joy. The patient continued to improve; that is, her anxiety abated.

My concern at his response was that emotional communication has to be based on genuine feelings. Should he be encouraged to use communications that cause so much conflict? I discovered through this work with his patients that he was working on a problem of his own, one of moral superiority, and he was enjoying the feeling with me. His patient had taken a backseat to his pleasure in feeling superior to his supervisor. I believe he finally gave it up when he had to either leave or try modern psychoanalysis. I was also convinced that when he tried it, it was his intention to prove me wrong. The fact that it worked despite this motive is testimony to the life force.

Does our belief that cure comes from the resolution of preverbal conflicts distort the way a modern analyst listens to patients? Does the modern analyst miss the oedipal manifestations and other interpersonal conflicts because of this preoccupation? One could! But not if one remembers that all relevant conflicts will enter the transference relationship if we stay in the "here and now," observing early roots only when they appear in the transference. I have found that it is not sufficient to explain real events or to arrive at an agreement on the patient's defense structure. While the narrative approach is part of the analytic journey, it is not the road from narcissism to object relations. We resolve resistances to verbalizing unconscious fantasies connected to the preverbal period of life as they are expressed in what we have described as the narcissistic transference. To be in a narcissistic transference-countertransference is to exist at the core of the patient as she relates to herself. Our willingness to go, with feeling, where the patient has trouble knowing herself makes the journey possible. If we agree that individuals are a part of nature—there, available for discovery, ready to be known—we can work analytically to reach this core. If the analyst can refrain from putting his own conflicts in the patient's space, remaining a twin image to the patient, the patient will take back the projected parts of the self, view the analyst as a separate person, and get to know herself.

Psychic Change through Group Analysis

Somewhere in what I am writing about is a theory of group treatment, but I won't address that theory directly.[4] Instead, I will address two questions: What in my life history may have influenced my becoming a group analyst and how do I do it? And what role does drive theory play in my work as a group analyst?

The story begins earlier, but let's start in 1944 during World War II. I was nineteen when my brother was killed on Guam, and my first short story was accepted by a Scottish literary journal. At that time I had not heard of psychoanalysis or group analysis.

That fall, instead of seeking treatment to understand the feelings aroused by my brother's death, I changed my major from literature to psychology and studied psychosis at St. Elizabeth's Hospital in Washington, D.C. After graduation in 1946, I entered graduate school in literature and taught freshman English to returning veterans. I did not return to psychology until 1950, when I was offered a research training position at the Psychological Corporation in New York City. Still I heard no one speak of psychoanalysis or group analysis. When I finished training at Psych Corp, I decided once again to leave psychology and in 1952 returned to write and edit, this time for women's magazines. I did not think about psychology again until 1955 when friends advised me to interview at the Theodor Reik Institute as a way of combining my interests within one field. In those days, it was not recommended that candidates training to be psychoanalysts undergo a group analysis. Slavson was training people, mainly social workers, to conduct therapy groups, but the analytic institutes emphasized individual analysis. I was encouraged to enter a three-time-a-week analysis while studying psychoanalysis, and so I did. After 510 hours of analysis and the completion of the psychoanalytic program, I decided to try a combination of individual and group treatment with Hyman Spotnitz. My analyst, Marie Coleman, and others spoke highly of him, and I had taken a course, "Diagnosis and Prognosis," with him. I had selected him as my control analyst from 1959 to 1961, so I was somewhat familiar with his work.

The first group I entered included some of my teachers from the institute. This was an odd situation for me because I had been in the habit, when with them, of putting my best foot forward. Now I was invited to speak meaningfully about my emotional life. I soon realized that I did not wish to do this. I preferred keeping my distance and presenting a pleasant picture of myself. I noticed that other group members had the same concerns that I did. They did not seem to want to do what we were ostensibly there in the group to do.

Learning the Meaning of Resistance in Groups

I learned by being in groups with Spotnitz in the 1960s, 1970s, 1980s, and 1990s when he closed his group practice that most of my fellow members had come with problems in their adjustment to others and they wanted the full attention of the other group members and the leader to help with their problems. Little by little we all learned that these desires were going to be frustrated, and when we were frustrated in the desire for special attention, we learned that each of us was aroused to action. We experienced impulses to get away, to punish, to hurt, to deny others our attention. We had the desire to destroy the leader and our fellow members, but each of us seemed also to have devices in our personalities that would hold these impulses in check, so usually we did not act on the more destructive of our impulses. Each of us defended against our more serious destructive tendencies in characterological ways. Our choices of defense were individually determined and different, but our impulses were remarkably similar. I noticed a correlation between the severity of the individual pathology in a group member and the strength of his drives. For example, a schizophrenic man raised the tension level of the group by his "bottled-up" appearance. We experienced him as a powder keg, yet on the surface his defenses kept him inhibited. He revealed no destructive attitudes towards us. He could blot out his connection to us and maintain a cold distance. He appeared indifferent to us, if not downright disdainful. I observed that Spotnitz appeared neutral in his communications and maintained what I later learned he called an *ego syntonic atmosphere*. He seemed aware of our drives and the defenses that each of us used, but I noticed that he did not describe these drives to us, nor did he interpret the meaning of our defensive behavior when the group was in a resistant state.

I learned a great deal from him and from group members about narcissism and its treatment. Emotional communications are much more effective than explanations of behavior. Spotnitz relied on group members to provide some of the emotional communications, and, after years of watching him, I realized that no analyst can offer all the corrective emotional experiences members need, so group treatment can be a real asset if members can supplement what the analyst can do.

I learned another important lesson from my groups with Spotnitz. The process takes a long, long while because group members tend to withhold the emotional communications needed by their fellows for cure. Resolving these resistances to cooperation will result in a group that is willing to be helpful, but it is preceded by a long period in which self-preoccupation must be worked through.

My own first group began in 1959. It included eight individuals who were already in individual analysis with me. My interest in group phenomena had grown as I worked to complete my analytic studies. I could not think of a psychology graduate program that interested me, so when I decided to work on a Ph.D., I discovered that New York University offered training in group dynamics. I completed a Ph.D. in group while completing my analytic training with Reik.

During this period, I developed a group practice with one or two groups each day. I observed many oddities. One was that most patients wouldn't say hello to fellow group members if they passed on the street for fear of "being improper." This view of groups emanated from Freud's (1912b) idea that the analyst is a mirror in which the patient sees her reflection. Most professionals assume that contact between group members outside the group is "against the rules." Some patients respond positively to this limited contact. Others fight against the rules, so I have experimented with "breaking the rules." I experimented with groups that included individuals who worked together and included members of the same family. I had groups in which I treated people who had faculty connections with each other in graduate schools. Some of my group members had been married to each other or engaged. I also had group members who never saw me or each other outside the treatment room.

By 1970, I was actively involved in developing institutes for the training of psychoanalysts. I continued to write and to conduct groups, but now I was writing about patients and training, particularly what I could understand from my work about drives and how they play out in individual and group settings. A little later, I prepared a chapter for *Treatment of the Narcissistic Neuroses* (Spotnitz and Meadow 1976) based on Spotnitz's work with group monopolizers and silent patients.

I remember the role of silence in one of my groups. Rather than act on destructive intentions, group members suppressed angry thoughts they experienced toward the leader or group members. One group member, Bette, had been to many analysts at our institute. She had enrolled as a student and left many times. Her analysts had never successfully dealt with the lack of gratification that she experienced as intolerable in the treatment setting. She returned to my group after a five-year absence, determined to "make it work this time." As in the past, she talked a lot but could not express negative feelings in the transference. The group resisted questioning her and, instead, joined her in stories about her outside life. She did complain about past analysts and failures of groups to help her, but after a year of talking, she fell silent. Several weeks later, during which she appeared glum and hardly ever spoke, she announced, "This is my last session!" She talked about how no one liked her or expressed any concern about her dilemmas and added that she found the group very dull. "You people are totally wrapped up in yourselves," she said.

The group members seemed stunned. "Why so sudden? This is too abrupt," they said. "Why had she never spoken of these feelings?" they asked. "Why hadn't she told them what she wanted? Would she reconsider?" As her complaints about them became more hurtful, it was clear that the group members were retreating. They were not going to express how they were feeling, particularly the murderous feelings that seemed to be building up. Finally, I said, "Forget it. Good riddance. Who needs such a hateful person in the group?" Again, group members appeared to be shocked. "How could I be so cruel?" they asked. But, one by one, they admitted that they, too, felt that she was an ingrate. They had listened patiently for months to her tales, and they had been sympathetic. Now what do they get but a slap in the face. They admitted that they had hated her silently for the past hour and that they had been irritated over the year when she rejected group involvement to tell stories about her life outside.

The last member to express his feelings said his main feeling was confusion. "I really like you," he told her. "How can I hate someone I really like? I need help with this," he told the group. I suggested that if that was what he needed, he could ask that we invite Bette to stay for two more sessions (the end of the month) to help him with this concern. Now it was Bette's turn to be shocked. "You mean," she asked, "that I can't stay longer than that if I wish?" Group members laughed when she said this. One commented, "We have just expressed all kinds of negative feelings that we feel you arouse in us. Why aren't you running for the door?"

I don't recommend that when a patient wants to leave a group that the analyst say, "Good riddance, you are a despicable person," but I have come to the conclusion that only one's own intuition will tell an analyst the kind of emotional communication that is needed. The reason I responded with strong negative feelings to Bette was twofold: I saw how frozen the group had become in the face of her affectless rage. I saw that she could paralyze a whole roomful of people. And I believed the intervention was correct for Bette as well as the group. If the nonverbal patient has only one option—to leave when he experiences destructive impulses—and he complains that there is no point in staying, that he can never get what he needs here, the group and the analyst need to treat this impasse as an emergency and deal directly with it as a treatment-destructive resistance. I had the idea that Bette did not like the group when she had negative feelings specifically because she did not believe the group could handle her negativity, and it was this belief that frightened her and caused her withdrawal. I surmised that both Bette and her fellow group members were suffering from the same fear—a fear of their own drives. What I really mean is, they suffered from a fear of an urgent desire to discharge destructive impulses in the group setting. To intervene around this issue dealt with both the patient's treatment destructive tendencies and those of the group.

Induced feeling states are the basis of what we sometimes speak of as the analyst's intuition. We know that group members and the analyst may experience similar feelings to those being experienced by a nonverbal patient in group. They may also experience complementary feeling states as those seen in the exchanges between a dependent infant and a caring or negligent mother. The feelings induced in the analyst may be fear of action or other feelings experienced by the patient. When the induction is complementary, the analyst may long to nurture or to control the expression of impulses to prevent their discharge.

The Role of Drives in Group Treatment

When I work back and forth from the individual to the group, I realize how frightened people are of their impulses. Group members are willing to give up feelings in order to avoid the actions they feel the urge to take when aroused. This poses a problem since the arousal of desires is a necessary part of the group experience.

This was another recognition I came to from my group work. When a patient does not experience early infantile longings in the transference, I must either rely on a group member to open the door to the unconscious, or I must admit that I am the wrong analyst for this patient. When feelings are fully expressed in a group setting, the roots of these feelings, the unconscious fantasy level, can be raised to consciousness. Longings based on drive states are enacted long before they are verbalized.

When a patient or the whole group is envious of one group member, this envy can operate as a silent resistance. Envy tends to appear repetitively and is expressed in subtle ways. Behind this fantasy may be the fantasy of the inadequate mother. This fantasy is then denied in favor of the fantasy that "I would be getting what I need if only she was not her favorite." However, once verbalized in group exchanges, envy can be integrated with the buried belief that the analyst is not quite loving enough to give what is needed. When patients are recovering from narcissism and beginning to feel separate, they recognize how much they need others to live. It is their rejection of this dependency that leads them to envy as a defense. "If I am independent and need no one, I will never be hurt. If the good qualities of the analyst were mine, I would be independent." Envy of group members protects a patient from that deeper fear that he can never be like the analyst or get "blood from a stone." Envy of siblings is more acceptable than the struggle to maintain satisfying and good internal object impressions. In the meantime, group members may act on sibling rivalry, replacing merger with the need for a separate other.

It would be tempting to analyze the defense of envy and relate it to early history, but that could only lead to an intellectual understanding. Traditionally analysts did this. They reconstructed the past with patients to explain their fears through memories. Groups can be much more emotional than that. Modern analysis follows the model of treatment in which conflicts can become active in the treatment room. This means that we expect impulses to be stirred up in the transferences. If we refrain from explanations, the arousal of desire will occur naturally.

We know that group inevitably entails action when longings are aroused. Pathology is the tendency to act out repetitively without remembering or knowing. Group can be described as acting out rather than thinking through. Drive theory tells us that our unwanted impulses are blocked from consciousness through emotional action. According to Ackerman (1961), group is an acting out form of therapy. He said that in the group setting the urge to act out conflicts is "natural."

The Narcissistic Transference

It is important to understand the role of the narcissistic transference in group work. Long-term groups lead us from oedipal enactments to preoedipal enactments, from the triad to the dyad to the split self. When a group functions at the formative stages of psychic development, a narcissistic transference will be experienced by the group members. In this stage, destructive impulsivity is a dominant force. The management of destructive impulsivity is of central importance when the group is regressed to preverbal levels. The analyst functions to create an environment in which desires can be freed from defenses and fully expressed in words without actions that would destroy either the group or its members. When impulses are verbally discharged, the ability to fantasize is restored. The group can be very helpful in exploring tensions and bringing longings to the surface to prepare for the exploration of individual and group fantasies. For a drive theorist, repressed fantasies originating in infantile perceptions, when clarified, free the patient to move to the primal unconscious. Those deeper longings when organized in language lead to cure.

In a narcissistic regression, the lack of a connection to objects is expressed first. Some of the statements made at that stage are a dislike for the group, the desire to get away, a feeling of being misunderstood. The discharge of these feelings leads to less desire for destructive action and more desire for contact with group members. Rumblings of the life drive begin with strivings for contact with others. It may be constructive urges that are aroused or the desire to fully experience life. Group members can be drawn slowly into the world of objects, but they pass through a number of stages from aloneness, isolation, and superiority in which they may express omnipotence, to twinning and subgrouping, to knowing themselves, and, finally, to living in a world with separate objects. If the drive theorist functions in a group without fear of the free expression of impulses and feelings, we have *agierte*, action on emotion.

When a group is struggling with narcissism, some group analysts emphasize the resistance of the group. Others concentrate on the individual patterns in each group member. I prefer to study individual patterns through the way the members interact during group sessions.

For example, I have a group of men who spent many years working through the narcissistic state. This group demonstrated the power with which the narcissist defends against recovery. When the group began, one member notified the others that there was no one in the group whose funeral he would attend. Another reported feeling isolated by the homophobic attitudes he felt from the group members. Most of the men felt "crazy" at times and expected loss of control.

A homosexual man, Dick, had, during the course of treatment, moved from promiscuous sex with strangers to a live-in relationship with a man that led to a settled family life. He shared little with the group because he felt they could not understand him. His history in individual analysis was to report periodic compulsive searches for a partner whenever he felt empty and unloved. He had always felt unloved, but when aroused, it turned quickly to raw anxiety, and that anxiety led to the search for a sex partner. He didn't give much thought to the compulsive attempts he made to rid himself of his unlovableness. Instead, he distanced himself and felt angry over the group's disapproval.

Another member of the group had for a long while been talking about his unlovable wife and his next-to-perfect mistress. All the men looked to him as a "father figure." He was thought of as the sex manager of the team. They never spoke of longings or the search for love with others. Their contacts, as they came out of narcissism, were of the macho sort, sharing exploits, competing, and exploring identity issues. The men were excited to be in each others' company. All were stimulated by the group and under intense pressure to act. They looked to each other as suppliers of the goods but feared connectedness on a feeling level. The steps they took toward intimacy were small indeed.

Working from narcissism to an interest in others is a difficult process that I am not sure I can describe. In this group it was the homosexual man who took the first step.

Dick returned from a summer vacation to report that for the first time in his life, he was loved and able to return that love. He described in detail how the man he had met made him feel "held." Other member spoke of their own extramarital relations. The longing to be touched emerged in their discussions of these contacts. Each of the group members described his desires and fears. Dick said he had "never been seen" by anyone before this summer. All revealed that not only did they long to be touched but to be held in someone's arms. For them this was an admission of a passive feminine part that had heretofore been rejected. The depths of the longings were frightening to them. They spoke angrily of the deprivation in their history and of parents who were unaware of their existence. They discovered that they had this perception in common. They all remembered that their fathers never touched them and that their mothers were seductive and overstimulating but made no meaningful connection with them as boys. The chorus rang, "I wasn't there; I didn't exist for them." Each reported feelings of isolation when outside the group and of pleasure when in the group. Some had found relief in their lives through sex and momentary feelings of union. Patterns varied from member to member. While some had become caretakers assuming responsibility for others and trying to be understanding, some stressed their independence and self-reliance. In transference to me they were tolerant. They worried about me, but usually they ignored me.

When Hal reported that he loved a woman from his workplace and that she loved him, it became clear that all were either acting outside the group or on the verge of action. At this time, the sex manager broke with his mistress. Both were married, and the contacts had become more and more difficult to maintain. When he announced that either he was changing or his wife was since the relationship was now better, the other men felt let down. That and the announcement by Joe that he was leaving his wife led to further anxiety and anger. Although the men agreed that they had terrible wives, this man's intended action frightened them. They thought he was going crazy. When he did not receive support from them, he told his woman friend that he was not going to be with her. He was going to work on his relationship with his wife.

As they opened up to each other, the talk changed in the group. Feelings heretofore rejected could be spoken of directly. They discussed the role of action in their lives. It had been the only way to achieve "being seen." The group members seemed to experience internal change as they spoke more directly about emotions. You remember, this was true for Bette also. Her defense of consistently interpreting her difficulties as interpersonal and caused by others led to her dislike of the group and desire to leave it. She had moved from chatting, to silence, to describing what was wrong with her group. When the group was released from its resistance to expressing their induced feelings and told her how she made them feel, she felt better and her fantasy life changed. For the men, competition and machismo gave way to an interest in acceptance and closeness.

Hal says he feels held by the girl at work. As the group that until now has used splitting and denying of passive feminine needs begins to admit to their rage at not being allowed these deep longings, we see a major shift. When they share the feeling that it is they who have denied their infantile needs, they recognize the deeper meaning of their wish to be touched.

In the transference to me, one group member says he no longer likes me. I was a rock for him until my husband died; now he has to take care of me. Because I am no longer there for him, he is disintegrating, and his fantasy is that I am a shattered rock.

Group members seem to experience internal change when they can participate in the resolution of a repetitive pattern within the group interaction. They talk more freely when they can help each other to control impulses, not having to deny them but having them in emotional language. As cooperative attitudes increase, patients help each other to talk directly about what each is experiencing.

For a drive theorist, repressed fantasies originating in infantile experiences when clarified free the patient to move to the primal unconscious. Those deeper drives when organized in language lead to the cure.

Dick still cannot understand why Hal does not want to go further with the woman who loves him and whom he loves. Hal says, In perfect union how can you go further? What about sex, Dick wants to know? Hal says he thought the reason the answer for him was not to have sexual contact with her was because sex was tied up with anger and destructive feelings. He has to keep union on another plane. Dick begins to see a connection between his longing for touch and his pursuit of new male partners. He has eliminated women from desire totally. He thinks they bring up too much anxiety. Joe, who wanted to leave his wife and settled for getting rid of the other woman, feels he was hurtful and was satisfied by the desire to punish someone if it could not be his wife. The actions have become verbal actions. Symbolically these men touch each other with their direct communication of feelings about unfulfilled longings.

As I have said before, drives or urges use what the environment offers in their search for discharge. The group analyst devotes himself to drive arousal and to organizing the drive seeking activities in language and genuine emotion. Eventually the group replaces the emptiness of narcissism and the desperation of action with words. I invited this group of men to let go of their macho postures, superiority, and competitiveness to know about their deeply buried need for love and relatedness.

Notes

1. Based on a lecture presented at the Center for Modern Psychoanalytic Studies' conference, "Through the Head or through the Heart," 1999 in New York City with Charles Brenner and Alexander Neubauer, published in *Modern Psychoanalysis* 25 (2000).

2. About the possibility of intrauterine mental activity, Gaddini (1987) writes:

[T]he mind's development is a gradual accomplishment advancing from body to mind, a sort of emergence from the corporeal which coincides with the gradual mental acquisition of a sense of physical self. . . . Long before it [the infant] has the capacity to assimilate phenomena from external reality, the individual mind is able to follow in what I would call a "focalizing" manner, the body's own functioning. . . . In any case there is no longer any doubt that mental activity is present and operational in the newborn, even if specific manifestations of it are difficult to demonstrate before the end of the second month of *ex utero*. (316)

3. Eros and Thanatos are defined as follows by Sternbach (1975):

In "Beyond the Pleasure Principle" Freud (1920) described the life drive as that which seeks to force and hold together, to unite the cells of living substance by an increase in tension, whereas the death drive opposes this tendency by seeking to abolish the chemical tensions which have created the living substance and by reducing or removing these internal tensions, it causes the eventual destruction and death of the organism. (321–22)

4. Based on a lecture presented at the Center for the Advancement of Group Studies' "Distinguished Guest Lecture Series," 1999 in New York City, published in *Modern Psychoanalysis* 24.

CHAPTER FIVE

~

Psychoanalysis in a Free Society

Is Violence Necessary?

Is this an age of violence? It is easy to think so. Terrorists die for revenge in Israel—there is genocide in Bosnia and Rwanda, serial killers, a Unabomber, 9/11, and the war in Iraq. In the United States we have seen an increase in the means of producing unprecedented bloody events.

This topic led me to the memory of my entrance into the age of the big wars. America had come through the thirties when the enemy was depression and poverty. When I thought of what followed, I began to wonder how and when one becomes aware emotionally of violence. World War II was, as I remember it, a time of expansiveness. Everything felt big. Important events were going on around us. Even as we read the news of Mussolini's rise to power in Italy, it seemed to have little to do with our recovery and growth in America. We heard bits and pieces of Stalin's destruction of those around him. We watched, or rather listened to our radios, as Hitler guided a whole population into unspeakable acts. Most of us listened in awe, still believing that these events had little to do with us. We thought that there were truly madmen out there. It was easier to see violence as external to us, the work of deviant minds with passive followers in an otherwise wholesome world.

By the time we entered the war in Europe, the quantity and character of violent acts had reached alarming proportions. We asked ourselves over and over how it was that so many people had followed their leaders in the commission of such abominable acts. We became armchair philosophers observing something we couldn't quite believe was true.

As Hitler came to power, Freud was living through the last seven years of his life. By 1933, his emotional awareness of aggression had been heightened by events in Germany. That year he wrote in "Anxiety and Instinctual Life" that he had been blind to innate aggression. He bemoaned his mistake in treating brutal acts as passing disturbances in mental life. He pondered why it had taken him so long to arrive at an understanding of the aggressive drives both in character and as they manifest in society. He said that "a belief in the 'goodness' of human nature is one of those evil illusions by which mankind expects their lives to be beautified and made easier while in reality they only cause damage" (104). Those who followed Freud (1920) in his acceptance of innate aggression added that the belief in purity leads us to seek perfection through the vilification of others. It appears that to believe his own earlier discoveries dating back to 1920, he had to first experience emotions connected with his daughter Anna's arrest by the Nazis and the anxious wait for her return. He had to experience the attempt to annihilate the Jews, the loss of friends, and, finally, for the second time in his life, lose his homeland as his friends and colleagues found the means to relocate him in London.

When Freud died, World War II had not really begun for Americans. If we were reading Freud at that time, we would read that the urge to destroy does not have to be taught. If we were thinking about this possibility, we nevertheless continued to confuse the patterns of violence with their causes. A postwar Broadway Show, *South Pacific*, summed up how we preferred to think of violence. In it was a song on the conflict between prejudice and love. It went, "You've got to be taught before it's too late, to hate all the people your relatives hate. You've got to be carefully taught." That is how we analysts prefer to think of aggression. We know that each of us uses relations with family, friends, and educators to learn the ways provided by our society and culture for the expression of destructive urges. However, it has proved dangerous to forget Freud's legacy that being taught whom to hate does not fully explain the violence we struggle with in our lifetimes.

During those last seven years of his life, Freud asked himself important questions about human nature. His writings turned to mythology and philosophy. He produced "Totem and Taboo" and in "Moses and Monotheism" wrote about the laws without which society cannot survive, including "Thou shalt not kill." He reminded us in "Civilization and Its Discontents" that we had yet to discover how to deal with innate aggression. He pointed the way for future analysts to understand aggression turned inward and externalized in the form of destructive actions. He rethought psychoanalytic theory and produced his most difficult work, "The Outline of Psychoanalysis," based on his dual drive theory. Given this last theory on human nature, he asked, "Is psychoanalysis of value? Is analysis terminable or interminable?" We ask, "Can psychoanalysis affect the problems created when men turn their innate aggression into actions directed against each other?"

Midway through World War II Americans were beginning to notice that the acts of violence they had been exposed to were not isolated aberrations. I awakened to the meaning of war at about the time that everyone else did. There were few young men on my college campus. They had been taken away as boys to serve in the war. I befriended a Japanese girl who was struggling over her separation from her family who were interned in the camps for Nisei, Japanese Americans, and her own relocation to the East. I was learning that to be German was bad; to abuse a German was acceptable, as I observed the abuse and impoliteness heaped on my German instructor by faculty and students, who, in hating Hitler, felt the need to hate him, too. In the midst of trying to understand a world very different from earlier fantasies of what it would be like at college, word came that my seventeen-year-old brother had been shot in the head and killed on the beach at Guam. My friendship with this Japanese girl ended abruptly when she learned of his death. Although we had tried to cope with events in her life, this particular lost life seemed to pose an irreversible threat to friendship. She asked, "Is it true?" and never really spoke to me again. When we passed on campus, she lowered her eyes and bowed. I didn't want to hate her or have her hate me. I wanted to be better, but it was too complicated, so instead I wrote my first depressed poem asking the meaning of life. Until then people had been good or bad. My view was reinforced every Saturday afternoon at the local cinema where, for five cents, I could see a double feature confirming that there are bad guys and good guys. The bad were always different. Their intentions were evil. The new complexities of right and wrong were difficult to absorb.

When America dropped the atomic bomb on two Japanese cities, all doubt ended of humans' innate destructiveness. Some accepted the rationalizations: it ended the war. American lives were saved, but to deliberately drop a bomb dead center on a city with 350,000 civilians to teach them, in President Harry Truman's words, "a lesson," instead of on a nearby military base with 40,000 Japanese soldiers? This was a new level of horror.

After the war, America was concerned with the storage of nuclear arms. It seemed imperative that we understand why our world might be destroyed. We asked ourselves again how it had been possible that we had watched the reign of Hitler in relative silence, turned a deaf ear to the Holocaust, and justified the bombing of Hiroshima as a necessity for our safety.

For a short time following World War II, we told ourselves we would profit from the lessons of history. We were beginning to pay attention to violence. In New York, intellectuals gathered in lofts and cafés to debate the use of power. Greenwich Village was a place to be because we were going to bring about change. Liberals and conservatives met together honoring freedom of speech as they voiced and heard each other's thoughts on violence, genocide and government power. Commissions were empowered to look in to these issues. In the universities, psychologists developed personality measures and the interest in anti-Semitism led to studies of prejudice. In 1946, Frenkel-Brunswick defined an anti-Semitic personality type:

- Expressing an admiration of power
- Making judgments based on stereotypes
- Seeing dangers as external rather than based on ego defects
- Integrating internally by projecting unacceptable impulse onto others

All these observations are true.

There was a brief time of hope, but it did not take long to remobilize the urge to destroy. In the early fifties, Senator Eugene McCarthy rose to political power by preying on the fear of communism. As chair of the Senate committee to investigate communism, he destroyed careers and families by the most casual reference to possible communist connections. In Hollywood, in government, and in the world of business, people lived in fear of being accused because of whom they knew. Many Americans left the United States during those years. I lived in Paris in 1953–1954 where two hundred thousand American expatriates poured over the European edition of the *Herald Tribune* as McCarthy wreaked havoc back in the States.

Eventually McCarthy left in disgrace, but again we did not have long to recover from that witch-hunt before another enemy had been found against whom brutality could be directed. This time it was the racially inferior, the blacks who had been kept at the lowest economic levels. Some scholarly studies attempted to prove lesser intelligence in blacks than whites. Through the promotion of "step 'n' fechit" imagery, individuals were encouraged in their degradation of this group.

By the mid-1960s, however, blacks had organized to fight back. In 1965, New York University, where I was studying, offered me independent study credits if I would go to the Selma Montgomery march. My department head encouraged me not to limit my study to the freedom fighters but to talk to the mayor, city planners, Head Start organizers, and those who came to the march. Driving south through Alabama, a pickup truck pulled in front of me and slowed his speed to thirty miles per hour. Ten or so miles down the road he pulled off at a farm house, and another truck pulled out doing the same thing. During that ride my sixteen-year-old daughter, her friend, and I expected to be killed.

Visiting the mayor turned out to be an equally alarming experience. I was escorted to a room and asked to wait. I waited for forty-five minutes. Then I tried the doorknob and found the door locked. After some anxious time someone, I think a sheriff, because he had bullets across his chest, took me to an office appointed in the French provincial style. The friendly mayor chatted—I wish I could remember what he said—then informed me that with his arm around my shoulder he would accompany me to the door for everyone to see. That would keep me safe until dark, he said, but I should be sure to be out of town by then. Of course, I went to the march. Driving out of town from the march, four young men pulled their car close to mine, revealed rifles in their laps, and while leaning on the window frame pointed in my direction. Now this was but one week in a life.

If we consider these experiences in relation to the experiences of the blacks, they are minor terrors in the overall picture, but I believe my chair did me a great service because this experience became a means to bring emotional understanding into my doctoral studies. What I had learned intellectually through the study of intergroup tensions required more direct knowledge of the life threatening experience that came from being identified as "one of them" as I traveled through the South. It taught me once again that we know nothing unless we experience events with genuine emotion. The lessons from World War II, from knowing McCarthy to the enlightening days spent in Alabama, were that the world cannot be changed by intellectual insights. To know violence, we must experience it as touching us in some way.

Freud's drive theory gave us a way to view the consequences when aggression is impeded from discharge. Freud (1933a) wrote, "It really seems as though it is necessary for us to destroy some other thing or person in order not to destroy ourselves, in order to guard against the impulsion to self-destruct" (105). Unfortunately, he did not live long enough to apply this theory of aggression to treatment; few analysts, social scientists, and certainly not the public at large chose to go along with his theory of a death instinct. A self-destructive drive was to remain incomprehensible for several more decades.

In the seventies, a handful of analysts applied dual drive theory to their observation of patients. They distinguished the pathological struggle between life and death forces in mental illness from the fusion of these forces in health. In their publications, they described some of the vicissitudes of narcissism. For example, Rosenfeld (1971) described patients who kill the loving dependent parts of themselves in favor of the autonomous unrelated self in order to maintain a sense of superiority and isolation. They wrote of other connections between the destructive drives and narcissism, and in so doing they brought many of the severe disorders within the purview of psychoanalysis.

I will leave the remaining lessons provided by the recent history of violence in America for readers to contemplate through their own experiences in the seventies, eighties, and nineties—events which most of you have been around to experience: the savagery of the war in Vietnam, the war between university students and university administrators, the struggles for sexual and political freedom in the gay liberation movement, and the more recent acts between the East and the West. During these decades, the young have debated the success of democracy and considered whether those with political power could have exerted more restraint in their use of aggression, but we find the continued need in us all for an enemy.

The lesson of history is that it is easier to ignore the depths of darkness in human nature. Lear (1996) in his article "The Shrink Is In," responding to the cancellation of the Freud exhibition at the Smithsonian, pointed out that if Freud is not given his place in history, it is not an attack on Freud or psychoanalysis but on the very idea that we have an unconscious. He suggests that only in a democratic society can an institution such as psychoanalysis exist to provide the free expression of ideas and values, and we agree that psychoanalysis and totalitarianism are incompatible. It is our hope that a society that encourages dialogue can provide the possibility for the constructive uses of destructive impulses. Aggression is inherent to our species, something we all share. If we think back over history, it probably evolved to its present form from man's hunt-and-kill pattern where the better hunter and his family survived. Now with aggression directed against our own kind, often we know not what we do. We do not experience our intentions subjectively as aggression but experience them as necessary acts for the general good or even for our own survival.

The social groups to which we belong provide acceptance of our points of view. For the most part, subgroups within society provide a common enemy against whom we can direct our hate, be it prolife or prochoice, the religious right or left. For at least two thousand years, denigration of the "other" before destroying him has been the *modus operandi* people use. By denigrating the other, the full recognition of our destructiveness, guilt, and shame is eliminated. Just as the Jews provided a common cause for Hitler and his followers as the object for externalization, so can our social groups be used to support either constructive or destructive urges. We have come to recognize that destructive impulsivity must find an out through pathological narcissism or an external enemy. Each of us seeks a group or cause toward which the destructive urges can be directed.

In this light, we should consider the many splits within the field of psychoanalysis. Schools of psychoanalytic thought have developed that emphasize the role of ego or self, society, or culture to interpret human behavior. In these approaches, what is seen phenomenologically is interpreted in various ways. The work done within these schools of thought is important because it directs our attention to where impulses can be acceptably directed. Nevertheless, a theory that leaves out aggression and the view that society is a product of our nature may limit our understanding of motivation to explanations based on a blank screen model, a screen on which parents lay down impressions. I grew up analytically in the age of the schizophregenic mother, so I learned that model very early. For modern-day analysts, a more complex view has emerged, a view supported by developments in neuroscience, a belief in an active rather than a receptive brain. Objects and things are cathected or attended to because they fulfill an individual's particular nature, not passively introjected. Cathexis, or attention to specific experiences, plays a major role in the process of selecting and shaping our experiences. We shape the environment according to need. It is this that makes psychoanalysis such an interesting field; it accepts the uniqueness of each of the individuals with whom we work. When Freud (1933a) shifted from the blank screen model to the active, imaginative mind that organizes its own experiences and to it added the dual drive theory, he provided the basis for the approach to our work that is described in the following pages.

Fusion and Defusion in Health and Aggression

When Freud died, the narcissistic neuroses and the psychoses were not considered treatable by psychoanalysis. With a deeper understanding of human destructiveness, psychoanalysts have been able to assist patients to fuse constructive and destructive drives. Freud (1924) and others have spoken of the motivating factor behind the patient's destructive behavior in masochism as aggression turned against the self. Freud saw masochism as the best evidence for the existence of a death instinct. When aggression is directed outward and is not fused with libido, as in sadism, it acquires its destructive character. We learned to think of primitive pathological responses as an expression of defused aggression. We connected narcissism to the inability to externalize destructive urges.

Clinical material confirmed that the schizophrenic, when he withdraws, blots out mental imagery and avoids affect and thought. In effect, he kills his mind. We also learned of a relation between somatic symptom and the inability to cope with thoughts and feelings when destructive urges press for expression. Yet we continue to be conflicted about whether urges to destroy are not exclusively a response to frustration. We find it difficult to say that while the way to destroy may be taught, urges are not. We are still engaged in Freud's struggle when he asked why it took so long to concede to a separate aggressive instinct. Now we ask, "Can we only survive as human beings if we turn aggression against the external world?" That was the last century's solution. We have studies that prove that prejudice in families is not a sufficient predictor of acts of violence in offspring. Neither are social conditions. Yet, on the other hand, we have studies that show that abused children become child abusers. We do know that a necessary condition of violent acts, regardless of circumstances or relations, is the arousal of destructive impulses and, further, that when these impulses are not turned inward, they seek individuals or groups against whom they can be directed.

When psychoanalysts work with behavior, as in discovering why a particular patient expresses extremes of prejudice, we discover what impulses are seeking discharge and we discover why the particular target was chosen. These are two very different kinds of interests. In the search for targets, we note how the social groups to which the individual belongs or his education in schools and family play a role in shaping the expressions of prejudice; when we consider the impulses seeking expression, we are examining the unfulfilled (unconscious) motives seeking satisfaction that form the patient's repetitive patterns.

An exercise in my grandson's kindergarten class is a modest demonstration of how education may feed hate and separation while attempting to educate. The topic was religious differences, the goal to teach tolerance of differences. The method of teaching was to ask each child what religion he or she was. Since many didn't know, they were asked to ask their parents. My grandson's mother confirmed that he was Christian, that she had been Christian, and that Papa was Jewish. The day I was next to visit, Zach seemed anxious for my arrival. He asked whether I would read to him after his father did, but when I got to his bedroom, he seemed to want to talk. "You are not part of us, are you?" he said. "What do you mean?" I asked. "You are not a Christian." He was tentative as he pronounced these words. I asked him what I was, and he said, with head lowered, "Jew." He appeared embarrassed. In the ensuing talk, he revealed that his teacher had said that Jews don't celebrate Christmas. Apparently this was the bad news! To him Christmas means presents, festivities, and holidays together. To not believe in it did not fit with his ideas about us, but it did worry him. I wondered about these complications children learn. Without talking, the fantasy of these differences can be buried and called upon to be rationalized as a reason for hating. I wondered how the children in his class were interpreting what they learned and whether they talked their young thinking through. The training my grandson and his friends are receiving may help them to choose whom to think of as 'not me,' but other requirements are mandatory for violent acts to occur. Violent action requires an intensity of destructiveness that cannot be contained in constructive actions, a conflict which can find no means of discharge in actions other than those directed to the destruction of another. I know that by the end of a week with Zach or a summer at Cape Cod, he has taken us in and that when the separation comes he tends to exclude us or forget us rather than be angry at the disruption. I hope he will be able to recognize the true injury we have done him rather than think of us as bad Jews.

Psychoanalytic Treatment

You may ask, How does past history, all of the above, apply to our work? What of psychoanalytic treatment?

To the extent that we find ourselves working with narcissism, we must learn to recognize the internal pressure to behave destructively. Observing patients we note that the intensity of the bottled-up condition determines the need to maintain the defenses contained while the level of fixation tells us the kind of violent acts the patient will be motivated to discharge.

There are many issues in the treatment of destructive impulsivity. Transference is our most useful tool. We have discovered that most of a patient's energy is directed toward those who are loved or needed. In the analytic room these needs can be displaced into the relationship with the analyst. The impulses may appear in narcissistic behavior, or they may be projected onto the analyst. In the narcissistic defense, patterns of discharge established prior to the development of language hold sway. To work through from primitive destructive impulses to language, action may occur in the transference as a prelanguage way of communicating. The fantasy solutions of infancy, particularly those first perceptual systems developed by the emerging self, are activated in the analytic room. Dreamlike solutions may be based on grandiosity, unity, defusion, or splitting. Most frequently in narcissism the patient annihilates the self in order to preserve an object field of the mind.

For those who come to us, analysts have a responsibility in their treatment to work for the freedom of each personality. They have a responsibility to avoid the temptation of setting life goals for their patients based on what they believe is good or of value. Each individual who learns his own nature will never be a blind follower. To free the patient in treatment, we should focus on how aggression is being processed, how the individual has organized impulses for both constructive and destructive actions, and whether these urges are directed toward the self or toward the other. We note patterns of fusion and defusion. We remember Freud's (1915d, 1920, 1923) edict that discharge is more important than object or pathway. We have the opportunity to observe, session by session, the circumstances under which urges to destroy will erupt. We have learned techniques for reducing the pressure for discharge by reinforcing infantile defenses as in the techniques developed by Spotnitz (1969, 1985), what we call *joining techniques*. We have become more expert in bringing defenses into focus, managing them until they are outgrown, rather than analyzing them. We do not let ourselves forget that when pathological narcissism is the mode of defense, destructive urges are constantly pressing for expression during the session. We have seen that the earlier the fixation the greater is the intensity of destructive urges turned inward. In conditions like impotency, we recognize the inability of the individual to integrate aggression with libido.

We observe other patients who use externalization or projection instead of the narcissistic defenses. We agree with Anna Freud (1949) that dangers from outside the psyche are much easier to deal with than internal dangers. In analyzing phobias and obsessions, she noticed that many defenses make internal dangers appear to be external. When we observe the agoraphobic's fear of venturing out, we look beyond the dangers in the environment to the temptations from within that arouse the patient's impulses that then press for expression. We find patients functioning, when they arrive for treatment, at different levels of development. Each patient can learn the fusion of drives at the level to which he is adjusted. As the patient masters developmental obstacles, he may learn more complex ways of coping with later urges that interfere with his ability to lead a satisfying and successful life.

Our work is to resolve resistances to the patient knowing herself, her thoughts and feelings. One of the principles that we sometimes forget is that analyzing resistances—that is, interpreting them to the patient—may not resolve them. It may lead to the patient bottling them up. Analysis attempts to unify instinctual opposites, not shut them away. When shut up, they turn to destructive acts.

Modern analysis has developed a number of tools in the quest for improved communication, using factual, object-oriented, and ego-oriented questions; using explanations when they facilitate communication; echoing the patient; overvaluing and devaluing him; and using first ego-syntonic and later ego-dystonic joining. If feelings can find their language, the distancing mechanisms found in narcissism and psychoses can be replaced by genuine self-connectedness. Positive and negative moments can be connected and find outlets. Urges and images, first projected, can be reclaimed, leading to the whole person who can successfully discharge aggression and love.

The greater enemies to successful living are pathological anxiety, deadness, and extremes of impulsive action. Our task is to resolve the blocks so that the individuals we treat can combine loving with hating. In each analysis, the analyst discovers the dark parts of her own nature. It would be difficult to argue that analysts do not also suffer from innate aggression for which they must find outlets in their daily lives. As I said earlier when describing how it was when I was nineteen, we want to think of ourselves as better than we are, but the desire for violent action is real and ever present within us. Even when we function as analysts, aggressive urges appear in each treatment that we undertake. If we know we are aiming for the triumph of the life force, we may be willing to free our patients from our tyranny and instead help them to find their own unique paths to fulfillment.

Nazi Germany has been explained as having a history of authoritarianism, a cultural phenomenon. Some saw genocide as inherent to the nature of totalitarianism. Jewish scholars traced genocide to a European history of anti-Semitism. The ordinary men of Hitler's Germany, described by Goldenhagen (1996) in his *Hitler's Willing Executioners* and Browning (1992) in *Ordinary Men* should alert us all to the importance of the talking cure. If we fail to recognize the power of drive, temperament, and energy, we do not have all the tools at our disposal to bring about the assertion of the life force. Goldenhagen credits the monstrous brutality of their acts to anti-Semitism, while Browning ascribes their acts to the theory that ordinary men can *become* acclimated to mass killing when given a rationale. This more complex explanation fits with the Freudian theory of unconscious destructiveness. Many answers have been advanced by psychoanalysts and psychohistorians to the question, "Why violence?"

Freud (1923) described the vicissitudes of aggression in personality when not fused with libido. We have witnessed in history some of the more horrible events that can occur when our violent urges turn to violent actions. We have learned that destruction can be turned on the self in suicide, depression, somatization, schizophrenia. And the bitter lessons of history are that humans are not always humane. In analysis, the impulse to hate grows to the point of action. In narcissism, it is the self that is destroyed. When the urge to act destructively comes to the fore during an analysis, the analyst has the task of providing a situation in which the patient, rather than attack himself, can experience the hate and discharge it in action that does not destroy either him or the analyst. During analytic sessions, the external world is the patient's immediate surroundings, the analyst and the analyst's office. As the other person present, the analyst learns that she is the focus of the patient's intentions to take action.

If we accept that the trouble in pathology goes deeper than a response to frustration (see Spotnitz and Meadow 1976), the alternative to severe mental illness is externalizing destructive impulses in constructive actions. Learning to feel hate impulses instead of anxiety and deadness is a first step. However, feeling hate with no outlet means the personality must shut down again. If we accept that everyone is violent, then it is violent behavior that is the problem.

An interest in the individual's inner life is our best weapon against our need to excuse violent acts. Each group interprets the history of killing according to that group's conceptualization of human nature. It seems relevant now that we each declare ourselves, at least to ourselves, and examine what we have experienced through the mirror of our own views.

Note

This chapter is based on a paper delivered at the National Accreditation Association for Psychoanalysis's conference "Psychoanalysis in an Age of Violence" in 1996, with Christopher Bollas, published in *Modern Psychoanalysis 22*.

Bibliography

Ackerman, N. 1961. Psychotherapy with the family group. *Science & Psychoanalysis* 9:150–57.

Alexander, F. 1950. Analysis of the therapeutic factors in psychoanalytic treatment. *Psychoanalytic Quarterly* 19:482–500.

Brenner, C. 1982. *The Mind in Conflict.* New York: International Universities Press.

———. 1991. A psychoanalytic theory of affects. *Journal of the American Psychoanalytic Association,* 39 (5):305–14.

———. 1994. The mind as conflict and compromise formation. Available: http://users.rsn.com/brill/egoid.html (accessed 5 December 1999).

———. 2000. Neonate and mentation. *Modern Psychoanalysis* 25:23–27.

Brenner, C., and J. A. Arlow. 1972. *Psychoanalytic Concepts and the Structural Theory.* New York: International Universities Press.

Browning, C. 1992. *Ordinary Men: Reserve Police Battalion 101 and the Final Solution in Poland.* New York: HarperCollins.

Edelman, G. M. 1992. *Bright Air, Brilliant Fire: On the Matter of the Mind.* New York: Basic Books.

Escalona, S. K. 1963. Patterns of infantile experience and the developmental process. *Psychoanalytic Study of the Child* 18:197–243.

Fenichel, O. 1953. *The Collected Papers of Otto Fenichel.* New York: Norton.

Ferenczi, S. 1924. *Further Contributions to the Theory and Technique of Psychoanalysis.* New York: Brunner/Mazel.

Fink, B. 1997. *A Clinical Introduction to Lacanian Psychoanalysis.* Cambridge, Mass.: Harvard University Press.

Freud, A. 1936a. The application of analytic technique to the study of the psychic institutions. In *The Writings of Anna Freud: The Ego and the Mechanisms of Defense*. Vol. II. New York: International Universities Press, 1966.

———. 1936b. The mechanisms of defense. In *The Writings of Anna Freud: The Ego and the Mechanisms of Defense*. Vol. II. New York: International Universities Press, 1966, 42–53.

———. 1949. Notes on aggression. In *The Writings of Anna Freud: Indications for Child Analysis and Other Papers*. Vol. IV. New York: International Universities Press, 1968, 60–74.

———. 1953. Instinctual drives and their bearing on human behavior. In *The Writings of Anna Freud: Indications for Child Analysis and Other Papers*. Vol. IV. New York: International Universities Press, 1968, 498–527.

———. 1954. The problems of infantile neurosis: Contribution to the discussion. In *The Writings of Anna Freud: Indications for Child Analysis and Other Papers*. Vol. IV. New York: International Universities Press, 1968, 327–55.

Freud, S. 1893. Studies on hysteria. In *Standard Edition*. London: Hogarth, 2:3–309.

———. 1895. A project for a scientific psychology. In *Standard Edition*. London: Hogarth, 1:283–397.

———. 1896. Further remarks on the neuro-psychoses of defense. In *Standard Edition*. London: Hogarth, 3:157–85.

———. 1899. Screen memories. In *Standard Edition*. London: Hogarth, 3:301–22.

———. 1901. The psychopathology of everyday life. In *Standard Edition*. London: Hogarth, 6:1–279.

———. 1905a. Fragment of an analysis of a case of hysteria. In *Standard Edition*. London: Hogarth, 7:3–122.

———. 1905b. Three essays on the theory of sexuality. In *Standard Edition*. London: Hogarth, 7:125–245.

———. 1906. My views on the part played by sexuality in the aetiology of the neuroses. In *Standard Edition*. London: Hogarth, 7:269–79.

———. 1909a. Analysis of a phobia in a five-year-old boy. In *Standard Edition*. London: Hogarth, 10:1–149.

———. 1909b. Notes upon a case of obsessional neurosis. In *Standard Edition*. London: Hogarth, 10:153–318.

———. 1910a. Leonardo da Vinci and a memory of his childhood. In *Standard Edition*. London: Hogarth, 11:59–137.

———. 1910b. "Wild" psycho-analysis. In *Standard Edition*. London: Hogarth, 11:221–27.

———. 1912a. Papers on technique: The dynamics of transference. In *Standard Edition*. London: Hogarth, 12:97–108.

———. 1912b. Papers on technique: Recommendations to physicians practicing psychoanalysis. In *Standard Edition*. London: Hogarth, 12:109–20.

———. 1913. Papers on technique: On beginning the treatment. In *Standard Edition*. London: Hogarth, 12:121–44.

———. 1914a. On the history of the psychoanalytic movement. In *Standard Edition*. London: Hogarth, 14:3–66.

———. 1914b. On narcissism. In *Standard Edition*. London: Hogarth, 14:69–102.

———. 1914c. Papers on technique: Remembering, repeating and working-through. *Standard Edition*. London: Hogarth, 12:145–56.

———. 1915a. Instincts and their vicissitudes. In *Standard Edition*. London: Hogarth, 14:111–40.

———. 1915b. Papers on technique: Observations of transference-love. In *Standard Edition*. London: Hogarth, 12:157–71.

———. 1915c. Repression. In *Standard Edition*. London: Hogarth, 14:143–58.

———. 1915d. The unconscious. In *Standard Edition*. London: Hogarth, 14:159–215.

———. 1916–1917a. The development of the libido and the sexual organizations. In *Standard Edition*. London: Hogarth, 16:320–38.

———. 1916–1917b. Introductory lectures on psychoanalysis: The libido theory and narcissism. In *Standard Edition*. London: Hogarth, 16:412–30.

———. 1916–1917c. Introductory lectures on psychoanalysis: The paths to the formation of symptoms. In *Standard Edition*. London: Hogarth, 16:358–77.

———. 1916–1917d. Introductory lectures on psychoanalysis: Transference. In *Standard Edition*. London: Hogarth, 16:431–37.

———. 1917. Mourning and melancholia. In *Standard Edition*. London: Hogarth, 14:239–60.

———. 1919. "A child is being beaten": A contribution to the study of the origin of sexual perversions. In *Standard Edition*. London: Hogarth, 17:177–204.

———. 1920. Beyond the pleasure principle. In *Standard Edition*. London: Hogarth, 18:3–64.

———. 1923. The ego and the id. In *Standard Edition*. London: Hogarth, 19:3–66.

———. 1924. The economic problem of masochism. In *Standard Edition*. London: Hogarth, 19:157–70.

———. 1926. Inhibitions, symptoms and anxiety. In *Standard Edition*. London: Hogarth, 20: 87–174.

———. 1930. Civilization and its discontents. In *Standard Edition*. London: Hogarth, 21:57–145.

———. 1933a. New introductory lectures on psycho-analysis. In *Standard Edition*. London: Hogarth, 22:3–182.

———. 1933b. Why war? In *Standard Edition*. London: Hogarth, 22:197–215.

———. 1937a. Analysis terminable and interminable. In *Standard Edition*. London: Hogarth, 23:211–53.

———. 1937b. Constructions in analysis. In *Standard Edition*. London: Hogarth, 23:255–69.

———. 1940. Outline of psychoanalysis. In *Standard Edition*. London: Hogarth, 23:141–207.

Gaddini, E. 1987. Notes on the mind body question. *International Journal of Psychoanalysis* 68:315–29.

Goldenhagen, D. J. 1996. *Hitler's Willing Executioners: Ordinary Germans and the Holocaust*. New York: Knopf.

Green, A. 1999. *The Work of the Negative*. Trans. Andrew Weller. New York: Free Association Books.

Grünbaum, A. 1984. *The Foundations of Psychoanalysis: A Philosophical Critique*. Berkeley: University of California Press.

Hayman, A. 1989. What we mean by "Phantasy." *International Journal of Psychoanalysis* 70:105–14.

Isaacs, S. 1948. *Childhood and After: Some Essays and Clinical Studies*. London: Routledge & Kegan Paul.

Klein, M. 1946. Notes on some schizoid mechanisms. *International Journal of Psychoanalysis* 27:99–110.

Lacan, J. 1977. *Ecrits: A Selection*. Trans. Alan Sheridan. New York: Norton.

———. 1981. *The Four Fundamental Concepts of Psychoanalysis: The Seminar of Jacques Lacan*. Book XI. Ed. Jacques-Alain Miller. Trans. Alan Sheridan. New York: Norton.

———. 1991a. *The Seminar of Jacques Lacan: The Ego in Freud's Theory and in the Technique of Psychoanalysis, 1954–1955*. Book II. Ed. Jacques-Alain Miller. Trans. Sylvana Tomaselli. New York: Norton.

———. 1991b. *The Seminar of Jacques Lacan: Freud's Papers on Technique, 1953–1954*. Book I. Ed. Jacques-Alain Miller. Trans. John Forrester. New York: Norton.

———. 1993. *The Seminar of Jacques Lacan: The Psychoses, 1955–1956*. Book III. Ed. Jacques-Alain Miller. Trans. Russell Grigg. New York: Norton.

———. 1998. *The Seminar of Jacques Lacan: On Feminine Sexuality—The Limits of Love and Knowledge, 1972–1973*. Book XX. Ed. Jacques-Alain Miller. Trans. Bruce Fink. New York: Norton.

Laplanche, J. 1999. *Essays on Otherness*. New York: Routledge.

Lear, J. 1996. The shrink is in. *New Republic* 21, no. 326:18–25.

Lefort, R., with R. Lefort 1994. *Birth of the Other*. Trans. Marc DuRy, Lindsay Watson, and Leonardo Rodriguez. Chicago: University of Chicago Press.

Lipton, R. J. 1977. The advantages of Freud's technique as shown in his analysis of the "Rat Man." *International Journal of Psychoanalysis* 60:255–73.

McDougall, J. 1978. Primitive communications and the use of countertransference—Reflections on early psychic trauma and its transference effects. *Contemporary Psychoanalysis* 14:173–209.

Meadow, P. W. 1996. Selected theoretical and clinical papers. *Modern Psychoanalysis* 21.

———. 1999. The clinical practice of modern psychoanalysis: An interview with Hyman Spotnitz. *Modern Psychoanalysis* 24:3–19.

Neubauer, P., and A. Neubauer. 1996. *Nature's Thumbprint: The New Genetics of Personality*. New York: Columbia University Press.

Nobus, D. 2000. *Jacques Lacan and the Freudian Practice of Psychoanalysis*. New York: Routledge.

Piontelli, A. 1992. *From Fetus to Child: An Observational and Psychoanalytic Study*. New York: Travistock/Rutledge.

Pollack, R. 1999. *The Missing Moment: How the Unconscious Shapes Modern Science*. Boston: Houghton Mifflin.

Rosenfeld, H. 1971. A clinical approach to the psychoanalytic theory of the life and death instincts: An investigation into the aggressive aspects of narcissism. *International Journal of Psychoanalysis* 52: 169–78.

Spotnitz, H. 1969. *Modern Psychoanalysis of the Schizophrenic Patient*. New York: Grune & Stratton.

———. 1976. *Psychotherapy of Preoedipal Conditions*. New York: Aronson.

———. 1985. *Modern Psychoanalysis of the Schizophrenic Patient*. 2d ed. New York: Human Sciences Press.

Spotnitz, H., and P. W. Meadow. 1976. *Treatment of the Narcissistic Neuroses*. New York: Manhattan Center for Advanced Psychoanalytic Studies.

Sternbach, O. 1975. Aggression, the death drive and the problem of sadomasochism: A reinterpretation of Freud's second drive theory. *International Journal of Psychoanalysis* 56:321–33.

———. 1990. Freud and the classical technique of psychoanalysis in a historical perspective. *Modern Psychoanalysis* 15:149–67.

Stone, L. 1954. The widening scope of indications for psychoanalysis. *Journal of the American Psychoanalytic Association* 2:567–94.

Strachey, J. 1934. The nature of the therapeutic action of psychoanalysis. *International Journal of Psychoanalysis* 15:127–59.

Szasz, T. 1965. *The Ethics of Psychoanalysis*. New York: Basic Books.

~

Index

group, 3, 10, 50, 55, 56, 65, 80, 83, 84, 85, 86, 92, 97–106, 112, 115, 120
group analysis, 83, 97
guilt, 8, 26, 63, 114

hallucination, 14
hate, 4, 24, 26, 30, 70, 100, 110, 111, 114, 116, 119, 120
Hayman, A., 87
Hitler, A., 109, 110, 111, 114, 119
hysteria, 28
hysterical, 15, 33

id, 82, 84, 90, 91
imaginary, 11, 12, 14
incorporation, 57
induced feelings, 38, 78, 105
induction, 74, 95, 101
infantile sexuality, 16, 21
interpretation, 16, 19, 25, 55, 68, 70, 77, 78, 82, 87, 95
introject, 8
introspection, 36
Isaacs, S., 86

Jewish Board of Guardians, 4, 55, 91
jouissance, 12, 14, 18, 21

Klein, M., 25, 26, 86, 87, 88, 91

Lacan, J., 11, 12, 13, 14, 17, 18, 19, 20, 21, 83, 87
language, 5, 8, 9, 10, 11, 13, 14, 18, 19, 25, 32, 33, 34, 35, 39, 40, 42, 43, 47, 48, 54, 56, 64, 78, 83, 86, 88, 89, 91–95, 103, 105, 106, 117, 118
Laplanche, J., 14–18
Lear, J., 114
libido, 3, 23, 30, 49, 50, 77, 115, 118, 119

Lipton, R. J., 78
love, 3, 4, 14, 24, 27, 28, 30, 34, 35, 52, 55, 60, 70, 75, 86, 104, 106, 110, 119

masochism, 20, 23, 28, 48, 49, 82, 115
McDougall, J., 91
memory, 10, 15, 17, 49, 54, 74, 78, 80, 81, 95, 109
modern analysis, 4
motivation, 2, 7, 31, 36, 60, 63, 64, 76, 77, 78, 90, 115

narcissism, 2, 3, 4, 28, 61, 62, 70, 71, 75, 77, 79, 82, 86, 87, 92, 93, 95, 97, 99, 102, 103, 104, 106, 113, 114, 115, 117, 118, 119
narcissistic defense, 70, 71, 76, 77, 78, 117, 118
Neubauer, P. and A., 88
neuromuscular, 33, 39, 40
Nobus, D., 20, 21

object protection, 23, 42
object relations, 39, 86, 92, 97
obsession, 28, 67
oedipal conflict, 20
oral drives, 8, 15, 33, 51, 54, 57, 63
orgasm, 90
Other, 12–21, 26, 27, 35, 44, 74, 81, 104

paranoia, 49
paranoid, 31, 37
pathological defenses, 26, 88, 96
pathology, 6, 8, 9, 18, 19, 26, 30, 49, 52, 59, 63, 74, 76, 98, 120
perception, 39, 42, 53, 59, 68, 69, 78, 87, 90, 95, 104
pervert, 21
phobia, 57, 66

~

About the Author

Phyllis W. Meadow, Ph.D., is a clinician, educator, researcher, and author. She is founder and chair of the board of trustees of the Center for Modern Psychoanalytic Studies and the president of the Boston Graduate School of Psychoanalysis. She is also a former president of the Society of Modern Psychoanalysts. She has served on the board of directors of the National Psychological Association for Psychoanalysis as membership director and was a founder of the National Association for the Advancement of Psychoanalysis. She is the editor of Modern Psychoanalysis and the author of the monographs Emotional Education: The Theory and Process of Educating Psychoanalysts and Selected Theoretical and Clinical Papers. Dr. Meadow is the coauthor with Hyman Spotnitz of the book Treatment of the Narcissistic Neuroses and has also written numerous published papers on psychoanalytic research and drive theory. She is in private practice in New York City and Boston.

Dr. Meadow has been highly influential in bringing contemporary psychoanalysis from the privacy of the consultation room to a profession concerned with the interplay between character and social issues. By working to create degree programs and relevant legislation, she has helped establish psychoanalysis as a separate profession. She has also opened training opportunities for women in psychoanalysis and written extensively on the role of destructiveness in character development.